A WORLD IN FLAMES
CIVILIANS

Neil Tonge is a successful children's author steeped in a love of history. His books include a wide range to cater for all ages and tastes.

Also available from Macmillan

A WORLD IN FLAMES: AT SEA
Peter Hepplewhite

A WORLD IN FLAMES: ON LAND
Neil Tonge

A WORLD IN FLAMES: IN THE AIR
Peter Hepplewhite

A WORLD IN FLAMES
CIVILIANS

NEIL TONGE

Illustrations and maps by David Wyatt

MACMILLAN CHILDREN'S BOOKS

First published 2001 by Macmillan Children's Books
This edition produced 2002 by The Book People Ltd,
Hall Wood Avenue, Haydock, St Helens WA11 0UL

ISBN 0 330 48297 1

Text copyright © Neil Tonge 2001
Illustrations copyright © David Wyatt 2001

The right of Neil Tonge to be identified as the
author of this work has been asserted by him in accordance
with the Copyright, Designs and Patents Act 1988.

3 5 7 9 8 6 4 2

A CIP catalogue record for this book is available from the British Library.

Printed by Mackays of Chatham plc, Chatham, Kent.

CONTENTS

INTRODUCTION

At 11 o'clock on Sunday 3 September 1939 listeners to BBC radio were told that the Prime Minister was going to make a speech on the radio. Very few people had television sets then and everyone relied on the radio for their news. All over the nation, families gathered around their wireless sets.

At 11.15, the Prime Minister, Neville Chamberlain, began to speak. His voice was tired and very solemn. He had previously warned Germany that Britain would declare war if their leader, Adolf Hitler, did not withdraw his troops from Poland. Hitler did not even bother to reply. As a result Britain was at war. It was an announcement that was to change everyone's lives.

Less than one year later, France lay defeated and Britain stood alone against the might of Nazi Germany. It was to be a struggle in which everyone, including women and children, would have to play their part.

World War II was the first 'total war'. Women and children were in the front line, whether they were helping with the war effort or being bombed in their homes.

You will read six extraordinary stories from the thousands of people that endured the horrors of a war waged against civilians as well as the armed forces.

• Ann Stalcup is only four years old when evacuees arrive in her village. Will the bombs drop on Lydney too?

• Many children are evacuated overseas, but prowling U-boats are determined to sink all Allied ships. Will young Kenneth Sparks survive the sinking of the ship *The City of Benares*?

• Anyone foreign comes under suspicion during the war – even those who came to Britain seeking an escape from Hitler's tyranny. Martin Goldenberg, a Jewish refugee, is interned in a camp.

• Pastor Donald Caskie stays in France to help Allied servicemen escape from occupied France – but the Gestapo is closing in. Will they capture him?

• On the night of 14 November 1940 the largest assembly of German aircraft aim to bomb Coventry into destruction. Will the city survive?

• In January 1945, on the bleak Polish/German border, a group of prisoners of war try to save the life of a young Jewess. Can they protect her from the Nazis?

A CHILD'S WAR

BATTLE BRIEFING

Between the end of June and the first week of September 1939, 3,500,000 children were moved from the town and cities, which were likely to be bombed, to live with families in the countryside.

Parties of schoolchildren clutching gas masks, their addresses on a label around their necks, made their way by train and bus to reception areas, shooed along by teachers. Some were upset; others thought it a lark and an adventure.

In the reception areas there was often chaos, for so many evacuees had not been expected. In one part of the country the authorities had to open schools and other public buildings to house them and even then there were no blankets or beds. Mothers (evacuated with children under 5) and children had to live on apples and cheese for four days and slept on straw.

Many of the children came from poor areas. One little girl

talked in whispers because she couldn't believe the luxuries in the house where she was staying. She was given a toothbrush, which she'd never had before. There was hot water when she'd only been used to cold. There were clean sheets on the bed and carpets on the floor. This was all very odd and more than a bit scary for her.

Whilst some of the children had a whale of a time in the glorious weather, others were desperately homesick. By Christmas many had returned home, for the expected bombing had not taken place. But when the savage Blitz bombing began a few months into 1940 a second flow of evacuees from the cities took place.

Again, when Germany switched her attack to Russia, the bombing grew less and the children returned home. The final and most terrible scramble came in 1944–45 when the 'flying bombs' began to fall on Britain.

This story opens with the arrival of evacuees to the village of four-year-old Ann Stalcup.

Date: 3 September 1939
Place: The village of Lydney, England

A Dark Beginning

Ann had heard the grown-ups whispering the word 'war' more and more often. She tried to find out what it meant 'to be at war' but her mum and dad had quickly changed the subject. They still smiled but didn't laugh as much. Whatever it meant it was clearly something very serious and worrying.

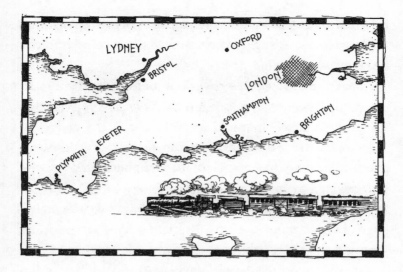

The village of Lydney where Ann lived.

However, little seemed to have changed for Ann initially. Her dad was a teacher and so he didn't have to go away from home like some of the other children's fathers and fight in the war. Nor was Ann sent 'somewhere safe', for the Stalcups lived in Lydney, a small town in the heart of the country. They had no need of bomb shelters like those who lived in the cities.

At first there were small changes. Ann's mum stuck wide strips of gummed paper across the windows in diamond patterns. Her mum explained that if a bomb dropped near the house, the sticky tape would stop the glass flying everywhere and hurting someone. Then her mum put up thick black curtains over the windows. It seemed such a shame to shut out the bright, sunny days of August but at night when the lights were put on the curtains were pulled tightly together.

'That's to stop the German bombers seeing where to drop their bombs,' Ann's mum told her as she wrestled to hang the heavy material on its hooks at the windows. 'We have to be especially careful,' she continued, 'because Daddy has to go round and check that no one is showing any light.'

Ann's dad had just become an air-raid warden. Every night he patrolled the streets, hammering on people's doors if the tiniest chink of light was showing.

As the evenings grew darker, Ann and her mum worried. So many people had been injured in accidents because the streetlights weren't switched on that they feared for her father's safety.

The Evacuees

'Ann, we'll be late for the evacuees,' said her mum. 'Remember – the children from the cities. They're being sent to the countryside away from the bombs. Come on now. They'll be tired and hungry.' And in the middle of this explanation, Ann was whisked inside her coat and bundled out of the front door.

By the time they arrived at the railway station, the train had already pulled in alongside the platform. Like a great exhausted dragon, the engine was sending off billows of steam as carriage doors were opened. Bewildered and frightened and tearful children emerged from the clouds of steam. Some clutched brown paper parcels tied with string, containing a few precious reminders of home. Some were no older than Ann and were desperately looking around for a friendly or familiar face.

No one really knew what was happening. Billeting officers were scurrying around trying to create some sense of order out of the dense crowds milling around on the platform. But things had gone badly wrong. Children had merely been put on the first available train. The officers were becoming more and more frustrated as they tried to match the children with the names on their lists.

All of the children wore labels around their necks with the name of the school and their name and address written on it in large block capital letters. The local people had assembled to 'pick' their evacuees. Farmers selected robust-looking boys, richer ladies looked for girls of ten to twelve who could lend a hand with the housework. Everyone went for the well-dressed children first, leaving the ragged and dirty ones till last. Many of these children did not have shoes, or had a cheap version with cardboard soles. Few had changes of clothing and some had even been sewn into their underclothes.

Some elderly unmarried men suddenly found themselves the 'parent' of four or five children. In other cases there were too many evacuees for the homes and they had to be put up at community halls. There were no blankets for them and hardly any food.

'Mrs Stalcup?' The billeting officer strode towards Ann's mother, a clipboard held in his hand.

'Yes,' answered Ann's mum.

'This is Judy and Jackie, your evacuees.' Two girls, one dark, the other blonde, peered out from behind the billeting officer's back, smiling nervously and clutching small brown suitcases.

Ann liked them instantly. They were big girls but it would be great fun to play with them.

'And, er . . .' the billeting officer hesitated for a moment, 'this is Miss Thomas, who's also been assigned to you.'

Miss Thomas looked as though a smile was completely strange to her. She was encased in a brown tweed jacket and skirt. Not one disobedient strand of hair strayed from her felt hat, which was pulled so tightly on to her head it looked like a soldier's steel helmet. Grasping her suitcase with both hands she defied anyone to wrest it from her. Her lips were narrow and closed as tight as a zip.

Almost instinctively, Ann backed away as if faced by a dangerous animal. Peering from behind her mother's back, she just caught Miss Thomas expel a noise, unrecognizable as a word.

'Hmmphhh. Disgusting. Expected to travel for hours without food or water and no . . . erumph, ahem . . .' she searched for the politest word she could find for a toilet, 'no ladies' convenience.'

Not long afterwards, Ann's four-year-old cousin Audrey and another evacuee called Edna, who was five, joined the Stalcup household. Ann was delighted for she had now two friends her own age to play with and her days would have been perfect if it had not been for the dreaded Miss Thomas. She complained about everything.

Ann's dad tried to keep the peace. After all, they all had to make sacrifices now there was a war on but even his patience was stretched to the limit and he would be increasingly heard to mutter under his breath 'Miss Dreadnought' whenever she steamed into view. Dreadnought was the name of a battleship in World War I.

Mealtimes gave Miss Thomas the opportunity to go through her lists. War clearly had only broken out in order to give her the most distressing and disagreeable time.

'Mr Stalcup, you will appreciate as a teacher that I need to study without disturbance. I would be most obliged if you could restrain your daughter's boisterous play between 5 p.m. and 6 p.m.'

'Mrs Stalcup, I'm sure you are aware that I bear a heavy duty in discharging my responsibility to the children. It is essential that I obtain sufficient rest, yet I find the bed that I occupy to be too soft for relaxed body posture.'

'Mrs Stalcup, I appreciate that we must all make sacrifices whilst there is a war on but I believe this can be done without serious damage to my digestion.'

'Well,' thought Anne, 'at least we don't have to put up with her at school. Poor Jackie and Judy.'

The Phoney War

For a long time after war was declared few bombs were dropped and many of the evacuated children began to drift back home. Jackie and Judy went back to Birmingham after six months and soon after, Audrey and Edna left too. Unfortunately, Miss Thomas stayed for twelve long, complaining months. Not a day passed without a mutter or a moan until one glorious day in autumn 1940 she got her come-uppance.

Delicately stepping through a mud-splattered farmyard, she tried to avoid a particular wet and sticky patch by stepping on to a metal grate covering a flooded drain. The grate collapsed and down she plunged until she was waist-deep in water. Struggling and muttering, she hauled herself to her feet, dripping wet and caked in cow dung.

Ann's mother looked at the smile appearing on Ann's face but quickly warned her daughter to behave herself. Later that evening though, Ann heard her dad roar with laughter and knew her mother must have just finished telling him the story of Miss Thomas's accident.

Government posters like these were used to encourage parents not to bring their children home from safety.

Gas Practice

Ann began school when she was four and a half, walking the mile and a half each day with her two cousins, and then on her own when they left to go home. The first few minutes of the day were spent in practising their gas drill. Many of the boys would pretend to be pigs and ran round snorting into their masks and because their faces were covered it was not always easy for the teacher to know who was making the noise.

By the summer of 1940 the war was going badly. Norway, Denmark, Holland, Belgium and France were invaded and occupied by the German army. Refugees fled their country and many came to stay in Britain.

Ann's village received a very special guest. Queen Wilhelmina of Holland, her daughter Juliana and Juliana's husband, Prince Bernhard, came to live in Lydney. The village was very excited and everyone tried to catch a glimpse of the Dutch royal family. Ann could barely contain her excitement for she knew that they would be attending church that Sunday.

Craning her head to see above the congregation, she was deeply disappointed. How could they describe themselves as royal when none of them were wearing crowns? And as for Queen Wilhelmina, she was wearing an ordinary suit and not a beautiful flowing gown!

A teacher takes her evacuees through a lesson.

Is My Dad a Hero?

Ann sometimes felt a little guilty that her dad didn't go to fight. As a schoolteacher he was in what was called a 'reserved occupation'. These were jobs the government thought were important and should not be interrupted. Instead, her dad helped the war effort as an air-raid warden in his spare time.

But all children want their dads to be super-heroes fighting the enemy single-handed. When Ann heard of other children's dads fighting in Africa and India she was jealous. But there was nothing sadder when one of Ann's classmates arrived in class wearing a black armband. This meant one of their family or relatives had been killed in the war. And, besides, Ann finally decided, her father was doing important work – watching for German planes as they followed the nearby Severn River up to Birmingham where they dropped their bombs.

And if there was any doubt left in Ann's mind about the courage of her father it melted away one night. A German plane had crashed nearby and one of the airmen parachuted to safety, landing in a field opposite Ann's house. Ann stared out of the window, terrified, as her father strode up to the German. Although the airman was shaken by his ordeal, Ann's father had no idea whether he was armed and would put up a fight.

Her father, however, seemed to have no fear. In his gentle voice he reassured the young man and then brought the young German into the house. He can only have been about eighteen and the family agreed that it was hard to think of him as the enemy.

'Perhaps,' Ann thought, 'some of the German people don't want this war either.'

From Saucepan to Spitfire

In wartime everyone was expected to help, even the children. Ann's mother joined the WVS and spent her days knitting scarves, socks and woolly hats for British soldiers. If a troop train stopped at Lydney station Ann's mother and the WVS ladies would be there on the platform, dishing out gallons of hot tea.

Ann soon discovered that she could help too. One

Children collecting aluminium to turn into aircraft.

night the BBC announced that everyone could help to build Spitfires by collecting old metal or giving money. They even listed what the money would buy. A rivet costs as little as 6d (2 and a half p), £22 would buy a bomb (this was the amount Ann's dad earned as a teacher). £2,000 would buy a whole wing.

But Ann was too young for pocket money and so she joined lots of other children searching for reuseable metals. Some of the boys would drag their bogey carts from door to door asking for any old scrap. Saucepans were particularly popular because they were made from aluminium, the same material as aeroplanes.

A New Sister

In the winter of 1942, Ann's mother had a baby girl. Ann was not impressed. 'Babies are pretty useless things,' thought Ann, 'until they are old enough to play properly, that is!'

There was so little baby equipment that everything had to be second-hand or borrowed. Ann's new sister's cot was made out of a cardboard box. Every night she was put inside a special baby gas box which had a plastic window at the top so the mother could look at her baby. The baby did not take kindly to being cooped inside such a smelly box, however, and screamed blue murder.

Food was always in short supply, for many of the ships bringing goods to the country were sunk by German submarines. As a result food was rationed.

Each person was only allowed two ounces (56.7 g) of butter per week, four ounces (113.4 g) of sugar and four ounces (113.4 g) of meat. If you were a farmer, however, then you had little trouble in getting hold of these price-less foods.

Having a new baby, however, meant extra rations in the house – powdered eggs, thick syrupy orange juice and powdered chocolate.

Ann's family could also add to their stock of food by following the government's advice to 'Dig for Victory'. People were encouraged to grow their own vegetables in gardens and allotments. Ann was lucky, for they had a

Children as well as adults did their
bit to save scraps of food.

big back garden. Some of their neighbours even kept hens and pigs. Sometimes they gave Ann's family eggs in exchange for kitchen waste that they could feed to their animals.

The Enemy

As the war dragged on more and more German and Italian prisoners of war began to appear in Britain. Some

Prisoners of war were sent to work on farms.

of them were housed near Ann's house. The strange
thing was that nobody was afraid of them. Although Ann
was only eight she blamed Hitler, not the prisoners, for
the war. Each morning they would be dropped off at
farms to work and then picked up in the evening. No
guards were needed.

Some people even welcomed the prisoners into their
homes and shared what little food they had with them.
Each day Ann and her mother would look out into the
field where one of the prisoners was working. One day,
Ann's mother cut a slice of cake, called him over and
watched him devour it. There were tears in his eyes as

he did so, and as Ann's mother turned to walk back into the house Ann could see the tears streaming down her face too.

Flying Bombs

Lydney, being a small village, escaped most of the bombing but one weapon invented at the end of the war terrified even those who thought they were safe. The V1 and V2 rockets were flying bombs launched from Europe, which could travel hundreds of miles unmanned until their engines cut and they hurtled silently to earth. Ann could hear them roar overhead but the worst moment of all was when the engines suddenly stopped. Ann would lie rigid in bed until she heard the muffled explosions. None fell on Lydney though, because there were bigger industrial targets at Birmingham. Another wave of evacuees followed these bombs and Ann found herself sharing her home with new children.

V. E. Day

7 May 1945 was an exciting day for Ann. Her school had suffered some damage. Spent bullets littered the floor. One had even passed straight through one of the boys' desks. He swelled his chest with pride as if he personally suffered a narrow escape. How the school had suffered this damage no one knew for there had been no air-raid warnings the previous night.

At 11 o'clock all the children lined up in the hall. The

headmaster stood on the platform and announced that the war was over and everyone gave a great whoop of delight. The Germans had finally been defeated. Church bells immediately began to ring out. Five years of war had come to an end, and with it most of Ann's childhood.

Ann now lives in America, a retired teacher.

FIGHTING FACTS

Evacuation

There were three periods of large-scale evacuation:

1939 The Phoney War period when bombing was expected.

1940 The Blitz when the Germans turned their airforce on to the towns and cities of Britain.

1944–45 When the flying bombs were launched against England.

Over three and a half million people left their homes even before the war was declared. All these people had to be housed. Volunteers went from house to house in safe areas checking who had space in their houses. You could not refuse. In return for accepting a single child you received 52p a week. Teachers looked after the children during the day.

They call this spring

Many children evacuated from the town had never been

in the country. When asked where eggs came from some thought it was pigs and others cows. Some were amazed that apples grew on trees and not in boxes and that cows, which they'd only seen in pictures, were bigger than dogs. Others picked flowers by their heads, thinking the whole stem would come up. One child wrote home, 'They call this spring, Mum, and they have one down here every year.'

Those that opened their homes to these children were sometimes appalled by what they discovered. The bewildered youngsters often just stared at knives, forks and spoons not sure what they were for and had no experience of hot meals or green vegetables. In the slums, mothers would usually hand their children a slab of bread and margarine, which they would eat standing up or running about in play.

Nor were some used to sleeping in a bed. One anxious lady tiptoed into the bedroom to see if the evacuee children were all right, only to discover them sleeping under the bed. As one child said, 'The country is a funny place. They never tell you can't have no more to eat, and under the bed is wasted.'

Not all evacuees came from poor homes, however. Some evacuated children who were used to better comforts at home suddenly found themselves in damp labourer's cottages with only cold running water. But fresh air and good food soon made a difference to many of the thin, pale children.

Rationing

In January 1940 everyone had a ration book. Every time you bought sugar, bacon, butter, milk and clothes you gave the shopkeeper some coupons from your ration book as well as money. The shopkeeper kept these and then passed them on to the local authorities. Meat and tea were added soon after, and jam in 1941. At the end of that year the government introduced a points system. Each person was allowed food valued at 16 points per month. This varied depending how much of a particular food was available. Pregnant women and children got extra food, such as orange juice and milk, and workers who did particularly heavy work received an additional meat ration.

People grumbled but they were prepared to put up with it because they felt it was fair. In fact, some poorer people had a better diet than before the war. By 1944, the average diet contained 6 per cent more protein than in 1939.

Black market

Some people, however, bought and sold things secretly (on the black market) to avoid the restrictions. This was against the law even if you had money. Only the rich could afford to get more by eating at restaurants but even this loophole was plugged. In 1942 restaurants were not allowed to charge more than 25p for a meal and meals were restricted to one course!

LOST AT SEA

BATTLE BRIEFING

At the end of May 1940 offers to take in British children began to pour in from the United States of America and countries throughout the British Empire. By 4 July 1940

Children waiting to be evacuated.

The City of Benares on its way to Montreal.

the government had received over 211,000 applications from parents who wished to see their children safe overseas, far from the bombing. A shortage of shipping meant the scheme was slow to get underway but by early September 2,664 children had left Britain, mostly for Canada.

On 13 September, The City of Benares, flagship of the Ellerman shipping line, departed from Liverpool, bound for Montreal in Canada. Aboard were 199 passengers, of whom 90 were children, and a crew of 209. They were in convoy with many British ships and escorted by cruisers and destroyers of the Royal Navy.

Four days later, the weather turned filthy. The sea began to swell into waves 30 metres high and many of the children aboard became seasick. Rain hit the decks in icy squalls.

Far beneath the grey swell of the ocean, German U-boats

prowled the seas searching for prey. Hundreds of thousands of tons of shipping were at the bottom of the ocean as a result of their deadly presence, and Britain was suffering shortages of food and fuel.

The German U-boat U-48 was on patrol in these waters. Under the command of Captain Heinrich Bleichrodt they had scored many successes and were now trailing this convoy waiting for the right moment to pounce.

The Royal Navy was stretched to the limit and could not provide protection all the way across the Atlantic to America. Feeling that they were now outside the area of the main hunting packs, the Royal Navy signalled 'good luck' to the convoy and steamed back to Britain.

Captain Bleichrodt knew the moment had come for him to strike. He gave orders for the torpedo tubes to be loaded. Manoeuvring the periscope into position, he swept the horizon ahead and chose his target – The City of Benares.

'Fire!'

The torpedo left a silver stream in the water as it headed for the ship. The City of Benares was struck on the port side, well below the water line. She immediately began to ship water and in a matter of minutes she was sinking.

Some people were trapped below deck and stood no chance. Others scrambled for the lifeboats. This is the story of some of the heroic children who survived and helped others to survive the terrible ordeal.

Date: 17 September 1940
Place: The North Atlantic

Farewell

'Keep warm, Kenneth. Wear your overcoat.'

Kenneth Sparks' mum fussed around him, straightening his overcoat collar, brushing a minute hair from his sleeve and finally dabbing his face with a moistened finger to remove a microscopic smudge of dirt from his nose. He wished his mother would stop treating him like a child. He was twelve after all.

'Yes, Mum. Don't worry. I'll be all right.'

Kenneth knew that his mother was only fussing because she wanted to be so busy that she wouldn't think about Kenneth going on a 3,000-mile journey across the Atlantic to Canada. She also knew it would be the best for her son. Many of the streets around Wembley, where they lived, were devastated. Gaping holes in streets now existed where there had once been houses. And nearby a cinema had been hit killing scores of innocent victims.

Londoners were now seeking refuge underground. Station platforms were full every night with sleeping families. This was no place for her son Kenneth, decided Mrs Sparks, and so when the government announced that there was a chance for some children to be evacuated to the safety of Canada she applied immediately.

But it was so hard to be parted from her son. She gave him a last affectionate squeeze and bundled him on to the train for Liverpool. Kenneth leaned out of the window and waved furiously at his mother. She waved her handkerchief in return and just as he began to disappear around a bend in the track, Kenneth saw his mother dab her eyes.

He would miss her but there was too much going on around him for him to mope. He shared the carriage with six other children and their guardian – a teacher from a London school.

Kenneth liked the teacher from the moment he saw her. Miss Mary Cornish seemed unlike most of the other teachers he had known. Firstly, she was young. Until he met Miss Cornish, Kenneth thought it impossible for teachers to be young.

Secondly, Miss Cornish was very friendly and beamed a great smile at them all, reassuring them now they were cut adrift from their families. She invented games for them to play as their train steamed north to Liverpool and their great adventure.

Liverpool

The great port in the northwest of England was the main lifeline to the United States of America and Canada. Across the ocean came a steady stream of ships carrying essential supplies. Losses to the wolf packs of German U-boats, however, were horrifying and Britain was in danger of being unable to continue fighting the war because of a lack of war materials.

Kenneth knew little of this and would probably not have cared less. This was exciting. New places, new friends. He pressed his face close to the railway carriage window and rubbed a little porthole in the condensation through which he peered. Smog hung everywhere but the city was thriving. It was certainly as busy as the London he'd left behind.

New sounds and sights hit his senses as soon as they left the train and marched in a crocodile down to the port. One docker held up his thumb for good luck but Kenneth could not make out what he said in his heavy accent. Cranes turned like prehistoric creatures over the children's heads, whilst crates and boxes hung suspended from their jaws. The smell of oil mingled with the sharp, refreshing ozone from the sea.

Ships reared up from the wharves. But how, wondered Kenneth, could something so massive, made from thousands of tons of steel, possibly float on nothing more than water?

'This is it. *The City of Benares.* You're on the starboard side, Deck 2, Cabins 7–11.' Their guide, an officer from the ship, pointed up the gangplank and towards the stern.

Kenneth hauled his heavy suitcase up the steep incline, following hard on the heels of Mary Cornish, who showed them the cabins they'd be living in.

Kenneth threw his suitcase on to the floor and flopped on to his bunk. A broad grin spread across his face. At last, at sea! A chance to travel the oceans and explore new countries. He felt like the early adventurers who sailed out into new and uncharted oceans.

Life on the Ocean Wave

The evacuees soon settled into a steady routine. Lessons aboard ship were in the lounges. Miss Cornish was a delight. She took every opportunity to draw attention to the things around them and use these for her lessons. And she also cared for them – talking soothingly and reassuringly to those that were afraid or homesick. The children soon trusted her and came to regard her as a mother.

Tuesday 17 September had been just one of these ordinary days, broken in its routine only by the farewells they'd waved from the deck as the Royal Navy escort left them to steam back to England. The children had stared at the ships until they became no more than tiny specks on the horizon, before they merged with the grey skies over the Atlantic.

Miss Cornish did her rounds of the cabins as usual that night, tucking the little ones into their bunks and kissing them goodnight. She switched off the lights, said a last goodnight and closed the cabin doors. The children turned and snuggled deep into their warm blankets, secure in the care and love of their guardian.

But their world was soon to blow apart. Beneath the cold waters of the Atlantic, Captain Heinrich Bleichrodt was closing in on his prey. He had no way of knowing that there were 90 children aboard nor that this was an evacuation ship. He saw only the enemy ahead and was convinced that the sooner England was starved of supplies the sooner she would make peace with Germany. It was, in his mind, as simple as that. He had orders to hunt down British shipping and that is what he had been trained to do.

The captain aligned *The City of Benares* in the cross-threads of his periscope.

'No. 1 torpedo ready?' he said calmly.

'Ready, sir,' rapped the reply back to him.

'Fire!'

Like a silver fish the torpedo left the tubes and shot towards its prey. It was 10 o' clock at night and the watch on the ship, even if they saw the torpedo, would have no time to shout a warning.

Kenneth turned in his bed. The sea was beginning to swell into valleys and mountains, and hailstones were pattering on the portholes. But inside his cabin and beneath the blankets of his bunk he felt warm and at peace.

A huge explosion suddenly rocked the ship. The steel hull buckled at the impact of the torpedo and then collapsed inwards. Icy water poured into the ship's engine room, drowning everyone on the lower deck. There was no chance to escape and waves swept over the sailors as they attempted to climb the gantries to the upper decks.

Kenneth fell from his bunk at the explosion and the sudden lurch of the ship. Pandemonium broke out.

Muffled shouts were punctuated with the creak of splintering steel. Stampeding feet pounded the wooden decks as people rushed to the muster stations.

Grabbing his overcoat from the hanger beside his bed, he shouted to the other children to get out as fast as possible. Few had the time or the presence of mind to grab outside clothes and instead began to tumble out of the cabin in thin pyjamas.

The scene outside was frightening. There was no panic, but the milling passengers were desperately looking to the crew to give them instructions. Their eyes were wide and fearful. The officers tried to make themselves heard, ordering the passengers to the lounge to allow the children to embark on the lifeboats first.

Meanwhile, the crew were hammering at the pulleys and blocks to release the lifeboats into the water. The ship was sinking rapidly. The sea was already lapping the stern deck and the passengers and crew had to haul themselves up to the front of the ship by means of the handrails. Some lost their footing and tumbled through the air, crashing into the cabins and decks.

Others threw themselves into the sea and disappeared from view, unable to struggle against the mountainous waves. Launching the lifeboats became increasingly difficult as the ship began to list for they no longer had a straight drop into the sea. Those that reached the sea did so at a dangerous angle, tipping forward and spilling their occupants into the ocean.

Miss Cornish gathered her charges around her. She tried to check they were all there but the pushing of the passengers made this a difficult task. She could wait no longer and decided to save those whom she could by shepherding them into the nearest lifeboat.

The boat was packed to the gunwales. Forty other survivors, along with six children evacuees, pressed close together in the boat. They looked back to those who were attempting to get further lifeboats and rafts launched from the dying ship. Captain John Henderson looked down at the faces turned towards him.

'Take care of yourselves,' he called out as he turned on his heel and disappeared among the crowd of passengers, giving orders and hoping by his controlled manner to instil calm into the ship's company. He was not seen again.

The lifeboat Miss Cornish and Kenneth were in slowly inched away from the doomed ship and the shouts of those on board began to fade in the stormy night. One by one the ship's lights flickered and then vanished. Those in lifeboats could see a number of people struggling in the water but, soon overcome by the bitter cold of the North Atlantic, their frantic efforts at swimming ceased and they drifted into death.

Others clung to overturned lifeboats until their numbed fingers could hold on no longer. Slipping into the sea, they desperately tried to claw their way back. But it was useless. The stormy sea swept them away from the upturned hulls. Those that managed to reach the overturned boats simply did not have the strength to haul themselves up the slippery surfaces.

Meanwhile, the ship was sliding to her fate beneath the waves. Sinking stern first, the prow of the ship reared high out of the water and then, with a rush, plunged beneath the water.

The other ships in the convoy steamed on. These were the orders. Unless they were near enough to pick up survivors they must do their best to get clear of the danger area. With no Royal Navy ships on patrol they would all have to fend for themselves.

Abandoned to the Sea

Both wind and sea increased in violence. Water constantly swept over the bobbing lifeboats and they quickly became waterlogged. Some shipped so much water that, despite the frantic efforts of the crew to bail them out, they began to sink. Soon many of the survivors were sitting waist-deep in water and were drenched with spray. And all the while, they were being lashed with hail and rain.

Their clothing was sodden and it was impossible to keep warm. Most had only their nightclothes on, which stuck to their bodies. They huddled closer, holding each other tightly in the hope that they could generate some body heat. Most chattered uncontrollably, their limbs and teeth shaking vigorously.

The death toll steadily climbed. One man buried 24 of

the 32 persons in his lifeboat, reciting what he could remember of the burial service as he slipped them over the side. Finally, overcome by the strength of the storm, his lifeboat capsized and the eight survivors were thrown into the sea. They got atop the lifeboat as it turned over but, one by one, they slipped off into the sea.

Ten-year-old Edward Richardson tried to keep a spark of life flickering in the nurse aboard the lifeboat in which he rode the angry seas. When the dying nurse asked that someone cradle her head, little Edward clasped her in his arms and said over and over again, 'I can see the boats, nurse. It won't be long now.' Only fourteen of 38 people in his boat survived.

Thirteen-year-old Eleanor Wright, who was being evacuated from Sunderland under the government scheme, buoyed the spirits of 23 others in her lifeboat by telling them, 'Don't worry, the British navy won't let us down.' Only five aboard lived to see her promise come true.

Beyond Hope

The Royal Navy escort that had so recently left the convoy turned and headed back to the disaster area as soon as the distress calls were sent out. One by one the survivors were plucked from the sea, but the terrible death toll still mounted.

The lifeboat in which Mary Cornish and Kenneth Spark had found refuge had drifted away from the others and was barely visible above the mountainous waves, however. After searching for hours, the Royal Navy assumed they had been lost.

Meanwhile, they were fighting a battle against the elements. The seamen rigged up a canvas shelter in the bows and the six boys with their guardian, Mary Cornish, found some protection against the stinging hail. Mary was tireless in her efforts to save the boys. She encouraged them to sing a favourite of the times – 'Roll Out the Barrel' – and continually rubbed their arms and legs to keep their circulation flowing. Mary even invented her own serial stories to keep them alert.

There was little food aboard and they were soon reduced to one 'meal' a day – an eighth of a slice of peach and a biscuit spread with sardines. By the eighth day most people had made up their minds that there was no hope of rescue. The storm had died down but there was no water and their food was practically gone. Many were drifting into a tired listlessness that heralded death.

Kenneth's head was slumped forward on his knees. He was tired, cold and hungry. He shivered and pulled his overcoat tighter. His mum had been right. Not that she knew it had saved his life – up to now.

A droning sound overhead suddenly interrupted his thoughts. It sounded far away, like an insect buzzing against a windowpane. It sounded like an aeroplane engine but was that possible? They'd neither seen nor heard any rescue planes. They must have given up searching by now, he reasoned.

It took all his effort to stagger to his feet. He put his hand over his brow to shield his eyes from the glare of sea and sky. The plane was just visible, a tiny black speck on the horizon.

'Look! An aeroplane!' he shouted, trying to rouse the other survivors.

One by one they hauled themselves to their feet and through salt-caked lips tried to shout. Their attempts were feeble but by waving their arms they began to attract the attention of the aircraft.

The Sunderland flying boat swooped low over them with a roar of its engines, banked and then began to circle above. A parachute billowed from the aircraft's hold and a crate fell to the sea. But food wasn't on the minds of the survivors now. It was rescue.

Kenneth had been in the Scouts and he had an idea. He snatched his handkerchief from his overcoat pocket and began to semaphore the pilot.

'City of . . .' Kenneth began to spell out the name of the doomed ship. The pilot knew in an instant who they were and radioed the nearest Royal Navy warship to come to the rescue.

Homecoming

The survivors were so weak that they had to be lifted and carried aboard the warship. With warm food inside them and several good nights' sleep they began to revive as they steamed back to Liverpool.

They came back to a hero's welcome. Crowds

cheered as the ship docked and discharged its famous passengers.

Kenneth scanned the crowd. He hoped his mother would be there. Everyone was waving so frantically that it was difficult to identify who was who. But there, amongst the densely packed crowds, one woman waved more fiercely than the others, crying for joy. Kenneth grinned and waved back, his overcoat flapping in the strong breeze.

FIGHTING FACTS

Casualty list

When *The City of Benares* sailed for Montreal there were 199 passengers aboard and a crew of 209. In all 258 were killed, including 77 of the 90 children. Only 57 of her passengers survived the attack. Immediately after this tragedy the government stopped the overseas evacuation programme.

The City of Benares

The City of Benares was built in Glasgow in 1936 and was 485 feet long, with a beam of 62 feet. More used to the route through the Mediterranean and Suez Canal to India, she was taken over by the government for war service and put on the treacherous seas of the North Atlantic.

Lend-Lease

Britain was dependent on imports to keep her people from starving but in 1940, with most of Europe conquered by Germany, she was running out of vital supplies of food and weapons. She looked to the United States of America for help but that country was not at war and many Americans did not want to get involved in what they saw as another European squabble. Roosevelt, the American president, however, had a great deal of sympathy for Britain in her single-handed fight against Fascism. In March 1941 he did a deal with Britain. In return for bases in Britain's West Indian islands, the USA gave Britain 50 destroyer ships. These were vital to protecting Britain's merchant shipping.

Shortly after, all sorts of goods began to arrive in a half-starved Britain, such as dried eggs, evaporated milk, bacon, cheese and canned meat. These foodstuffs were crucial to keep the British people healthy. In 1941 one-fifteenth of goods came from America.

The U-boat Menace

Once Hitler had put off his invasion of Britain, he attempted to bomb and starve Britain into surrender. Early in February 1941, Hitler ordered increased attacks on ships bound for England and also on the ports. The German U-boats achieved spectacular results and Bristol, Liverpool and Glasgow were heavily bombed.

The Battle of the Atlantic, as it came to be called,

resulted in many deaths and lost ships. In the three months ending in May 1942, 142 merchant ships were sunk by U-boats and 179 by air attacks.

Tonnage of ships lost	
December 1940	300,000
February 1941	400,000
March	500,000
April	700,000

In April 1942 the government ordered the Ministry of Information to stop publishing the figures for ships lost as this was causing dismay at home.

The Allies learnt how to protect their ships better by going in convoy, and by using radar and depth-charge bombs. By 1943 the worst was over and Germany was losing more U-boats than she could replace.

WHO ARE THE ENEMY?

BATTLE BRIEFING

In 1939 there were 70,000 Germans and Austrians living in Britain. 55,000 of them were refugees who had escaped arrest and imprisonment in Nazi-occupied countries and had come to Britain for safety. Despite this, the government saw them as a risk to national security. Some were even afraid that they might be spies posing as refugees. They could not simply be returned to Germany, for they would face almost certain arrest and execution there. Large numbers of them were Jews who had been victims of Nazi racial attacks and wanted to help the British war effort.

One solution suggested by the government was to 'intern' the refugees; that is, to round up all foreigners and put them in camps under guard. But as many of them had already been victims of brutality this was decided against at first. Instead, 'enemy aliens' went before a committee who had to decide if they were Class A and should be imprisoned; Class B, which meant that they could not move more than five miles away from where they lived; or Class C who were free to go wherever they wished. As many aliens were also refugees they were put in category C.

When France fell to the Nazis in 1940 the British government got worried again and this time interned 2,000 male enemy aliens. Newspapers tried to whip up feelings against foreigners. One Daily Mail headline demanded, 'Intern the lot.' Some employers began to sack foreigners, whilst some local authorities turned them out of council houses.

When Italy entered the war in 1940, over 4,000 Italians were immediately interned. By mid-July, as the threat of invasion increased, two-thirds of all German and Austrian men were interned in camps.

Many of the internees were moved to the Isle of Man after short stays in temporary camps. Conditions in these

German nationals interned on the Isle of Man. In this photograph a group are returning from exercise.

The Isle of Man.

camps varied greatly. At Sutton Coalfield, they lived in tents pitched on damp ground. At Wharf Mills in Lancashire, they were housed in an old cotton mill, which was alive with rats. Husbands were separated from wives and neither were allowed contact with the outside world.

Those still allowed to live in their homes were under many restrictions. They were not allowed to own cars, bicycles or maps and had to be at home by nine o'clock every night.

Strangely enough this also included scientists who were

working in great secrecy on the atomic bomb. There was no alternative to using these refugees as British scientists were doing other vital war work. It had dawned on the authorities, however, that the vast majority of these 'aliens' were among the bitterest enemies of Nazism and they had talents which could be used in the war effort.

By August 1942 many 'aliens' had been released. By 1943 nine out of ten were at work doing highly skilled jobs.

Martin Goldenberg was one Jewish refugee in Britain who found himself interned.

Date: June 1940
Place: Isle of Man

An Unexpected Call

Martin Goldenberg just wasn't expecting it. Not here, not in Britain where he'd fled to safety from Austria. But there was the police sergeant at the farm ordering Martin to accompany him. True, the policeman was friendly, even a little embarrassed.

'I've got orders to pick you up. They want you in Barnstaple,' he said slightly apologetically. His voice picked up and became more authoritative. 'Take a tooth-brush with you and a piece of soap. You'll be back in a day or two anyway.'

In June 1940 there'd been a campaign against all Germans and Austrians living in Britain. France had fallen and the Nazis were poised less than 22 miles away across the Channel. Invasion scares were scudding around the country like storm clouds. These 'aliens' spoke German – the hated language of the Nazis – and this made many British people deeply suspicious of them. Who could tell if they were loyal to Britain or not? Perhaps they were spies or possibly turncoats who would side with the German army if they landed in Britain?

Why Us?

Martin had expected that some aliens suspected of being spies would be arrested. But where was the sense, he thought, in arresting people such as himself who had been amongst the first victims of the Nazis?

'Do you mind if I look through your belongings?' the police sergeant asked politely.

'That was a bad joke,' thought Martin. 'What belongings?'

Like all Jewish refugees, everything had been taken from him when he'd fled Germany. All he'd been allowed to take with him was an old battered suitcase and twenty reichsmarks (£5).

Martin had been studying medicine at the University of Vienna when the Nazis had marched into Austria. He was immediately thrown out of university for being a 'non-Aryan', not a pure member of the German race. His stepfather and stepsister, who were solicitors, were banned from practising the law. No Jew was allowed to go to school with Aryans and adults were forbidden to follow a profession, such as teaching, law or medicine.

Worse was to come. Jewish shops were attacked until the owners were forced to sell up at give-away prices. Jews were attacked in the streets and the authorities tried to humiliate them further by making them scrub the cobbled streets on their hands and knees. The Nazis were gradually dehumanizing the Jews, and many ordinary people did nothing to stop them.

Jewish people around the world tried to help. In Britain the Jewish community raised enough money and got permission to bring 600 children to England. Martin and his best friend, Fred Dunstan, were lucky – they were asked to come with them and look after them.

In March 1939, two dishevelled young men arrived in England with 600 bewildered children. They did not know where they would end up or whether they would see their families again.

Are We Safe?

One family took a particular liking to Martin and invited him and Fred for tea one day. As they sat round the table, Martin and Fred were astounded at the ignorance of the family, who seemed to have no idea what was happening in Germany. No idea that people were arrested in the middle of the night and taken to camps.

The son, who was a naval lieutenant in the Royal Navy, had been on a friendship visit to a naval base at Kiel in northern Germany.

'Absolutely splendid chaps,' he declared when describing the German officers he'd met. 'Thorough gentlemen.

45

We really ought to be friends with these chaps. They're just proud of their country. Once Hitler has helped Germany get back on its feet again, there'll be no more talk of war.'

Martin bit his tongue. He was a guest and he doubted they'd understand what was happening to Jews under the Nazis. He gave Fred a meaningful look.

Watching the British army on training exercises frightened Martin even more. Not only were many ignorant of what was happening on the mainland of Europe, but the British seemed totally unprepared to face the Nazi war machine. The soldiers were smartly turned out but their rifles were World War I models. Some were carrying cardboard cut-outs of tanks, and anti-tank guns for practice attacks. Martin worried about their ability to fight the Nazis when war broke out, as it was likely to.

Willing to Fight

After the children arrived and were sent off to schools in England, Martin volunteered for the army. His offer was turned down, however, and he continued to work with small groups of children.

Wherever he went, he was always made welcome. One day a strange event occurred, which helped him to understand the English better. As he sat round the tea table the conversation turned to foreigners.

'That there manager at Boots the Chemists. The cinema manager too! Foreigners, the lot of them. What's wrong with local people doin' them jobs.' The host's voice rose in anger.

Martin stared at his shoes, feeling increasingly uncomfortable until he realized that the man wasn't talking about people from other countries but from other counties in England. He was complaining about the number of newcomers from Lancashire and Yorkshire! He hadn't even thought of Martin as a foreigner.

When France fell in 1940, Martin felt even more afraid. England would be next. But again, Martin was surprised at the reaction of English people to this disaster. As old Charlie explained, the French had only held them back. Now they were on their own they would do much better.

'You don't understand us. Now we're rid of the French we're really going to go.'

Martin couldn't believe it. These island people, cut off from Europe, they really thought they could win the war on their own.

Under Arrest

Martin went willingly with the police sergeant, thinking that they would be back home within a day. In Germany it would have been different. The knock on the door in the middle of the night. Dragged off to a police station. Beatings. Perhaps execution or disappearance to a camp.

But this seemed so English – so polite, so jolly. The policemen's wives made sandwiches for Martin and the others that had been detained. But they still meant business and events began to take an unpleasant turn.

Many of Martin's companions were lecturers and pro-
fessors who had taught in German and Austrian univer-
sities. Before the Nazis had come to power they had
been honoured people but deprived of their jobs, they
had fled to England. Now they were being treated as
criminals once more.

Ordered to board coaches, they were driven to a former Butlin's holiday camp at Paignton which had been
converted to an internment camp. It seemed so strange.
Before the war these had been places where people had
their holidays. The sounds that echoed around the place
had been of children laughing, bands playing. Now an
ominous silence enveloped the holiday chalets and

Guest houses were taken over to form a
prison camp on the Isle of Man.

barbed wire enclosed the camp. Members of the local Home Guard stood to attention with fixed bayonets. As the internees marched past, Martin heard one call out, 'Why not shoot them right away?'

Martin stayed there for one week before he was transferred by train to Shrewsbury. He and his fellow internees were herded along the platform, they were marched through the town as if they were the enemy. Martin felt deeply ashamed and tried to hold his head high but then thought better of this attitude. They may mistake his pride for arrogance – the arrogance of Nazi conquerors.

But once clear of the town both the internees and the soldiers began to relax.

'Here take this, mate!' One of the soldiers passed his rifle to Martin.

Other soldiers took their cue from this enterprising soldier and began to off-load their equipment on to the shoulders and backs of the other internees.

As they marched into the camp, they were stared and scowled at by groups of German sailors. Anger swept through the ranks of the internees. No, they couldn't do this, not be imprisoned with Nazis. Outsiders would assume they were all one and the same.

Martin and a group of the internees decided they must speak with the camp commander immediately. They expressed their dismay that they would have to share a camp with the very people who had persecuted them back home. The camp commander listened patiently and replied that he would remove them as soon as he could. He kept his word and they were removed from the prisoner of war camp.

A Strange People

Life in the new camp was as good as it could be considering they were not allowed to go wherever they pleased. Quite often the food was better inside the camp than out. Amongst the internees were a large number of Germans and Italians who had lived in England for over twenty years. A good number of them had been chefs and so the food they prepared was truly magnificent. Even the guards would hand over their rations to be transformed into mouth-watering meals.

German nationals arriving at a camp in
the north of England.

They did not want for entertainment either. Jewish members of the Berlin and Vienna Philharmonic orchestras formed a camp orchestra and gave regular concerts. Professional actors too were amongst the detainees and they occupied their time staging plays. Some of the British officers even made a special trip to London to bring them costumes for the performances.

Martin had been in the camp a little over a week when they began to recruit the camp inmates for work on farms. No one was forced to work but it was a release from boring camp routines. Martin also felt that in a small way he was also helping the war effort. He loved being with the farmers and their families. Each day

Barbed wire around a camp
in Liverpool.

he'd be invited to share a meal with them and they'd soon be laughing and joking with one another.

Time and again Martin could not get used to the attitude of the British soldiers. Whenever they arrived at the farm, the corporal would ask the internees to give a whistle if they saw an officer coming because he would usually settle down to a peaceful snooze in the barn. How could such people defeat such a ruthless enemy? Martin simply had to shake his head in disbelief. But he also understood that these were people who would not be ordered around and would fight for this belief with their last breath.

Saluting an Enemy Alien

Martin was kept in the camp for only a short time because the British government decided to release internees for important war work. There had, of course, been no need to intern any of these people in the first place. Having escaped from Nazi tyranny they were not likely to help the enemy. But in the panic of 1940 anyone who was not clearly British came under suspicion. Perhaps it was excusable in this atmosphere of fear, and it quickly passed without long-term effects.

Martin immediately reapplied to join the army and because he was well-educated soon became an officer. Martin served throughout the war and when the fighting was over chose to make his home in this country. However, he could never get used to the idea that when he barked out orders to British soldiers he did so with a

German accent. And despite the fact that he was an officer, his identity card was stamped 'Enemy Alien'. But he never forgot that Britain had sheltered him when he was a refugee and treated him with respect when he was interned.

FIGHTING FACTS

We Are Refugees

Aliens were marched to Liverpool under armed guard. Onlookers often turned nasty and shouted insults at them. One group of internees sang, 'We are refugees: thanks for your hospitality' to the tune of 'God save the King' so that the crowds would realize that they had nothing to do with Hitler.

Ice Cream Wars

The Italians are justly famous for their restaurants and particularly for their delicious ice creams. At the entry of Italy into the war, however, Italian restaurants and ice cream parlours were attacked by mobs in London and elsewhere. Four thousand Italians who had lived less than twenty years in this country were interned. Some of those rounded up included those who were bitter enemies of Mussolini and his fascist regime.

Italians were never regarded with the same suspicion as Germans and many Italian prisoners of war worked on the land with very little supervision. By 1943 most Italian internees had been released.

Walls Have Ears

The government ran a huge campaign to persuade people to be careful what they said in case they gave information away to spies. Posters were put up everywhere. Newspapers were censored. As a result some of the wildest rumours began to spread throughout the country. One newspaperman warned his readers:

> *Do not believe the tale the milkman tells;*
> *No troops have mutinied at Potter's Bar.*
> *Nor are there submarines at Tunbridge Wells.*
> *The BBC will warn us when there are.*

Fear of Spies

Many aliens were rounded up because there was a fear that information was being passed to the enemy. Government campaigns reinforced this message with slogans such as 'Careless Talk Costs Lives', suggesting that there was a vast network of German spies in Britain. In fact, the few who reached Britain in the summer of 1940 were quickly caught and were not particularly clever. One pair who landed on the Moray coast in Scotland were rounded up at once when they failed to understand English pounds, shillings and pence. Another waded in from the sea dressed in hat, trench coat and a green suitcase, dressed, as he thought, in typically British clothes. And Karel Richter, picked up after landing by parachute near St Albans, was unable to explain why he was wearing three sets of underclothes.

Most internees were innocent civilians caught up in the war. However, three members of the 'Right Club' – from L–R Captain Maule Ramsay, Tyler Kent and Anna Wolkoff – were found guilty of passing on secrets to the Germans.

Isle of Man

The Isle of Man, lying between Ireland and Great Britain, was thought to be a secure place to keep internees before they could be sent overseas, mainly to Canada. Before this could happen, the British government set up transit camps run by the military until August 1940 when the Home Office took over. (The Home Office is responsible for people coming in and out of the country.)

Sadly, on 2 July, the *Andorra Star*, carrying fifteen hundred German and Italian internees to Canada, was torpedoed and sunk off the west coast of Ireland.

Making Music

Most refugees were sent to internment camps on the

Isle of Man but despite being separated from their families, they reported a holiday atmosphere on the island.

In Her Majesty's Prison

In August 1940, a peak number of 1,600 British subjects were detained in prison without trial, suspected of being sympathetic to the Fascists. Most were held in Brixton Prison where they amused themselves during the hot summer, playing the most famous of English sports – cricket. By mid-1941 only 400 were still detained.

The government passed laws to deal quickly with suspected traitors, which included the right to try people in secret. Several people were prosecuted. On the Isle of Wight a woman was sentenced to death for cutting military telephone wires, but her punishment was later reduced to fourteen years' imprisonment. A schoolteacher was jailed for saying Britain might lose the war to his pupils.

Sir Oswald Mosley

The leader of the British fascists, Sir Oswald Mosley, was arrested and imprisoned on 23 May 1940 in Brixton Prison. He and his followers wore Nazi-style uniforms and distributed **anti-Semitic** propaganda. He also gave powerful speeches and conducted hostile demonstrations in the Jewish sections of east London. His treatment at the hands of the prison authorities was very different from what happened to political prisoners in

Germany, however. Mosley and his wife were given a flat in Holloway Prison and were even allowed to employ other prisoners as their servants.

Lord 'Haw-Haw'

The Germans broadcast propaganda to the British, sometimes pretending that the radio station was actually in Britain. One of the most frequent broadcasters was an Englishman called William Joyce, whom the British nicknamed 'Lord Haw-Haw' – the sound a donkey makes. On one occasion he actually managed to cause disruption at a munitions factory in the Midlands by saying that the factory was to be bombed that night. Workers stayed away and production dropped. After the war William Joyce was caught and hanged by the Allies.

DOUBLE CROSS

BATTLE BRIEFING

In May 1940 German forces broke through the French army in the Ardennes and overran France in six weeks. The tiny British Expeditionary Force was forced back to the coast at Dunkirk where it was miraculously rescued by a flotilla of small and large craft and brought back to England.

Shortly afterwards the French asked the Germans for peace terms. The settlement was harsh. France was divided. There was an occupied zone, controlled by Germany and including Paris and the Atlantic coastline. The rest of France was run by the French themselves and governed from a small town called Vichy. Marshall Petain, the heroic general of World War I, was brought out of retirement and made head of state. He chose Pierre Laval as his Prime Minister.

Few Frenchmen at this stage of the war wished to con-

tinue the fight alongside Britain, particularly after Churchill
had ordered the bombing of the French fleet to stop it falling
into the hands of the Germans. Most thought it their patriotic
duty to serve the Vichy government or at least to keep their
mouths shut. As the Vichy government had not declared war
on Britain, it was easier for British people to move about the
unoccupied zone of France.

Some Frenchmen, however, hated the idea of their country
being at the mercy of the Germans and began to organize
resistance. At first, most of them were communists but as
disillusionment with the war spread, more and more
Frenchmen joined the ranks of the Resistance. Some blew up

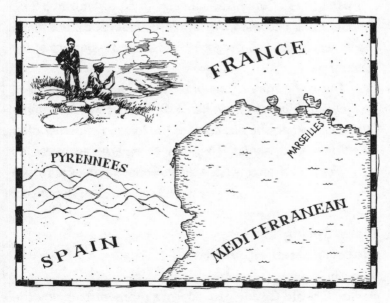

British soldiers and airmen were helped
to escape through Spain.

railway lines or passed information on to the British with secret radio transmitters. Anyone caught was likely to be shot.

Others resisted by helping British soldiers and airmen to escape back to England. Pilots in particular were valuable to the British war effort. They were expensive to train and in short supply. Through a network of contacts, escape routes were established through France and over the border into Spain. Spain was not in the war and once there the airmen were fairly safe. The Germans were infuriated at this breach in their security and the German secret police, the Gestapo, hunted down members of the Resistance ruthlessly.

By the time of the Allied landings in Normandy in 1944, the Germans occupied the whole of France. By this time, most Frenchmen had become enthusiastic supporters of the Resistance.

This is the story of one brave Scots minister who helped to get British airmen back home. So famous was his reputation that he became nicknamed 'The Tartan Pimpernel' after the fictional Englishman 'The Scarlet Pimpernel' who rescued French aristocrats from the guillotine during the French Revolution.

Date: Spring 1941
Place: Marseilles, France

Suspicion

Pastor Donald Caskie paused for a moment to enjoy the spring sunshine on his face. It had been a long, dangerous

The Scottish Church in Paris where Dr Caskie was Minister.

winter. Through his network of agents, he'd helped hundreds of prisoners of war escape through France and Spain, back to England. The Seaman's Mission hostel, which he ran, was an ideal cover for men to come and go without arousing too much suspicion. But the Gestapo weren't fools and they had come to the same conclusion. Pastor Caskie's days were numbered, for the Gestapo were closing in and he was being watched.

But he felt the work he was doing was too important to stop and so today he had an appointment with an agent, known to him only as the 'Patron'. He was to meet him outside Jean's café on the waterfront. He'd taken a long, roundabout route to throw the Vichy police off his trail and he hoped he'd succeeded, for

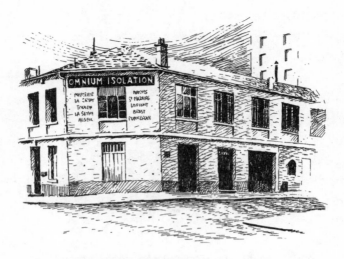

The Seaman's Mission in Marseilles where Dr Caskie organized the escape of many British airmen and soldiers.

many lives depended on him. He paused in front of a large shop window and as he lit a cigarette, shielding the flame from a cold wind that blew from the harbour, quickly checked to the left and right using the reflection from the plate glass.

He crossed the street and sat at an outside table, choosing to sit with his back to the cafe so he could survey the whole of the square in front of him. A man sitting at a nearby table joined him.

'Coffee, Donald?'

Pastor Caskie nodded and smiled.

'Cigarette?'

Donald took one and accepted a light. This was just all

too pleasant. The spring sunshine, sitting at a cafe enjoying a coffee. Donald's mind began to drift away from his mission.

'Donald!' Donald's companion brought him back to reality. 'Nine men will arrive tonight at 22.00 hours. They've come from German-occupied France but they've been given the very best identity papers so there shouldn't be any trouble. Oh! And they'll be escorted by one of our chaps. Cole. Used to be a Scotland Yard man but joined the army. As soon as he delivers them, he'll head back north again.'

Donald was worried. He didn't like the sound of this at all. The operation seemed too smooth and for this man Cole to return and bring more men along the same escape route seemed too good to be true. Were the Gestapo setting them up so the whole route and the agents that served it could be discovered?

'Patron' could see the doubt on Donald's face. 'Don't worry. This has been well organized.'

'Yes, but by whom,' thought Donald, 'our agents or the Gestapo?'

It was the last time they met. 'Patron', whose real name was Bruce Dowding, was arrested by the Gestapo several months later and shot.

Suspicions Aroused

The moment Donald met Cole he was suspicious of him. The man talked too freely about his personal life. No agent did this, for if arrested the less they knew about one another the less they could confess under torture. Cole also brushed aside the difficulties of the journey. Escorting RAF pilots through occupied France was full of danger, which no serious agent took lightly, and Cole seemed to be so relaxed about the whole mission.

Donald shared his doubts with Pat O'Leary, who commanded the underground escape routes in the south of France. Although the two men got on well, Pat did not share Donald's worries.

'I know he's a bit of a loud-mouth, Donald, but he got nine men here in one go. Not bad, eh? I know he's not the sort of chap that people take to but he's done his duty.'

Donald had no evidence to persuade Pat otherwise, but he remained deeply worried and on his guard.

The Betrayal

For a while, Pastor Donald Caskie buried his concerns in his escape work. Cole went north again and many escaped soldiers, sailors and airmen who passed through the Seaman's Mission arrived safely at their destinations.

The arrival of David was to change all that. He arrived at the Mission door one evening, having escaped a German prison camp, and tumbled in to the warmth within. The pastor was used to receiving men who had been tried to the extremes – foot-sore, so weary they could sleep standing up, hungry and filthy – but this young man was particularly nervous and edgy.

During the night the young man was unable to settle,

moaning and talking in his sleep. The next morning, the corporal who was in charge of these escapees explained his worries to the pastor and asked if he could talk to the young man and find out what was troubling him.

Donald asked David to do jobs around the mission which he willingly took on. Gradually the younger and older man became friends.

One evening, as they sat together, David talked freely of his village in Yorkshire and the mill in which he worked. As his conversation turned to the subject of his mother, however, he suddenly broke down in floods of tears.

'What's troubling you, David? We'll soon have you through Spain and back to England. You'll be sitting at your mother's fireside in no time.' Donald tried to comfort the man.

But David would not be calmed. Something terrible had happened and he must talk to someone. Donald bided his time and, as David's sleep became more and more disturbed, he decided to tell him that it had been arranged for him to leave the following night on an escape into Spain.

At the news David clutched his stomach as if in dreadful pain, but it wasn't a physical illness that he felt. He was tortured by a terrible memory.

'Tell me, boy,' pleaded Donald.

David looked up at Donald. His eyes were red and tears streamed down his face. 'I'll never go home. Never!'

Donald had seen this reaction before. Many of the escapees felt that they would finally run out of luck at this last hurdle.

'I have done a terrible wrong. That is why I don't deserve to return home.' David's face was grim.

'Tell me, David. Tell me what's troubling you.' The pastor took David's shoulders with his hands.

My Friend the Enemy

Piece by piece David's story tumbled from his lips. He had been taken prisoner shortly after the defeat of France. He was exhausted and near the point of collapse and worried about his mother.

In the prison camp he'd been unable to sleep. His heart ached to be back home in his small Yorkshire village with his friends from the chapel he attended. He found little friendship with the other prisoners.

One morning, as he was standing in line for the bread distribution, a German corporal spoke to him in halting English. They talked about their homes and, in the course of conversation, it gradually became evident that David and the friendly German belonged to the same religious sect. After this they became the best of friends.

The German corporal gave David extra bread rations and the best jobs around the camp. New huts were being built beyond the perimeter fence and the German corporal ensured that David was assigned to the work detail that was installing the plumbing. The young man was delighted with the prospect of a job indoors and saw immediately that it also offered him the possibility of escape.

Each evening the German guards would do a roll call before the prisoners were marched back to barracks. David waited until this was complete and then silently dropped out of line and under a wooden hut. As night fell he made a dash for the nearby fields and then joined the roadway which would lead him to the frontier and into France.

He'd barely covered a couple of miles when he saw a bicycle lamp in the distance heading in his direction. He began to panic, first darting behind a tree and then scrambling on his stomach behind a small pile of building rubble.

The cyclist passed safely by but then braked and dismounted. David was terrified and, pressing his body into the ground, raised his head to see what was happening. Coming towards him he saw the silhouette of a German soldier clutching a pistol in his hand. David searched for a weapon to defend himself with. He stretched out his hand and grasped hold of a narrow, iron fence post that lay in the rubble by the roadside. He tightened his grip around his weapon and as the soldier passed by, he sprang to his feet and brought it crashing down on the man's head.

The soldier staggered forward and moaned. David brought the iron bar down again on the man's head and then again and again. He could not stop. All his fear was coiled inside him and he needed to release it. Blow after blow followed until David saw the man was motionless. He'd killed him.

David was suddenly drawn to see the face of the man he'd killed and hauled the soldier over on to his back. As the moonlight broke through the clouds, David could see clearly who it was and it numbed all his senses with the horror he'd committed. Staring up at David were the lifeless eyes of the corporal who had befriended him and had provided him with the means of escape.

Donald tried to comfort the boy but, although his words helped, he realized that the young man had been wounded too deeply. 'Perhaps,' he thought, 'when he makes it back home to his village, amongst his mother and friends, he will, in time, be able to forget.'

Death in the Mountains

The next evening, Donald said his goodbyes to the soldiers and they set off with their guide to cross the Pyrenees into Spain. None of them made it. The Germans had been warned in advance and were waiting for them. David was shot dead, one other was seriously wounded and the rest were prisoners.

Donald was heartbroken but determined that the traitor needed to be found and dealt with. The guide had managed to escape capture and came to see the pastor.

'All would have been well if we'd followed the original plan but when your letter arrived, changing the route, we walked straight into the ambush.'

Donald looked puzzled. 'My letter? What letter? I sent no letter. You know I would never send a letter in case it fell into the wrong hands.'

Of course the guide could not produce the letter because he'd destroyed it so if he was captured he would not betray anyone. Donald knew immediately who the traitor was. Cole had known the inn where the men would assemble before the flight across the Pyrenees, the times of the border patrols and the route the escapees would take.

But again Cole escaped the finger of guilt. Pat O'Leary explained that Cole had an alibi for the night in question. He'd been travelling north to Paris and couldn't have known about the operation. But Donald's suspicions remained. It would have been easy for Cole to find out about the mission before he'd left Marseilles for the north.

Other agents, however, began to share Donald's suspicions about Cole, who managed to move so freely between occupied France and Vichy. The net seemed to be closing more tightly around their organization and arrests began to follow. Donald came under increased surveillance from the Vichy police.

Although suspicions were building up around Cole there was no hard evidence to convict the man. Pat O'Leary had Cole investigated and was satisfied that he was innocent. Escaped soldiers thought he was wonderful. The secret service in London said they had complete trust in him, but Donald could not shake his instinctive distrust of Cole.

A Friendly Word

A few days after the report which cleared Cole's name, Vichy French detectives surrounded the Seaman's Mission. They searched everywhere and questioned everyone but found no evidence to connect it with escaping prisoners. Not all the French detectives and policemen were happy working for German masters and they often warned people that the Germans were on their tail. As Donald showed the policemen the door, one detective who was in sympathy with the Allies turned to have a quick word with the pastor.

'Monsieur, I want to warn you about a certain gentleman who has a pretty girlfriend in Paris. She is very friendly with the Gestapo.' As he shook Donald's hand, he gave it an extra, meaningful squeeze.

This was the evidence Donald needed and he rushed to Pat O'Leary to relay the warning. Cole was due to arrive in Marseilles in a couple of days' time and the commander decided that the agent would be confronted with the evidence.

As soon as Cole arrived he was taken to O'Leary and cross-questioned. But he was a slippery character and demanded a proper investigation. He admitted having a girlfriend in Paris and said if it was true she was working for the Germans then he would stop seeing her but otherwise he was innocent. He stuck to his story even when Pat got tough with him. So adamant were his denials that the commander decided to send him into Spain and then back to England where he could be properly investigated.

That night he was escorted to the border and crossed the Pyrenees with some escaped RAF pilots. He led them straight into a Nazi trap and then fled north to Paris and the Gestapo.

Arrest

As soon as Cole's betrayal was known the Germans began a round-up of Resistance agents. Over 100 of the 150 that operated the escape route were arrested and thirty of them were immediately shot as spies. The others were sent to concentration camps in Germany where most met their deaths. Over 500 escaped prisoners of war who were in hiding along the escape route were also captured. Some of them were shot as spies because they were wearing civilian clothes.

Pat O'Leary managed to make a daring escape after a schoolgirl cycled through the night to warn him of the danger.

Donald knew it was a matter of time before they came for him and set about destroying any papers that might betray those who worked on the escape route. Most of the men in the Seaman's Mission were scattered to various safe houses throughout Marseilles, probably known to the sympathetic Vichy police.

One morning in May 1943 the police arrived to arrest

Pastor Donald Caskie. He was taken in a black, window-less van to police headquarters where a Vichy Military Tribunal awaited him. The judge read out a long list of charges. He was accused of being in touch with British Intelligence and helping enemy servicemen escape to England.

Donald was a brave man and faced his accusers courageously. 'If this is a Court of Law,' he said, 'where are your witnesses and what is your evidence against me?'

The judge could only produce vague accusations regarding the people Donald had been in contact with and it became evident that the court was embarrassed by its lack of evidence. They were also aware that many nuns and priests were friends of the pastor and news would soon reach the outside world if he was treated badly.

'How do you explain,' continued the judge, 'how so many men who were arrested trying to cross the fron-tier had passed through the Seaman's Mission?' The judge sat back, smiling triumphantly at what he thought was a winning point.

Donald stood up stiffly and addressed the Tribunal. 'I understand that those seamen had their papers checked by your policemen and they were satisfied that they were genuine. I can't be expected to be able to spot false papers if your own policemen fail to.'

The judge became more and more frustrated that he

was unable to pin any guilt upon Donald. He called the prosecution to a halt and informed Donald that they would retire to consider their verdict.

Over an hour passed before they filed back into the court. The judge stared at Donald. 'We find you guilty and you will be on probation. You must close the Mission at Marseilles and leave the city. We suggest you move as far away from the border as possible – to Grenoble.'

Grenoble

Donald was given ten days to pack up and leave Marseilles. After making sure all the arrangements were in hand to enable the remaining escapees to be guided to safety, he boarded a train for Grenoble, taking with him one battered suitcase and his concerns for the agents arrested.

Settling into a hotel in the city he soon found that his reputation had preceded him. It was not long before members of the Resistance began to contact him. With the memory of the traitor Cole still with him he took great care before he trusted his visitors.

This did not mean that he stopped taking risks. Once a month he was given permission to visit a prisoner of war camp at Nîmes to take a church service. Although the prison guards checked his papers carefully, they did not carry out a body search. Safely concealed all over his body were wire cutters, files and forged papers which he passed on to the officers in charge of the escape committees. It was here that he came across a most important RAF prisoner – Commander Whitney Straight, a Battle of Britain air ace. He'd kept his identity secret from the Germans, who believed him to be plain, ordinary Captain Whitney.

His true identity was revealed to Donald who passed the information on to the British secret service. Whitney Straight became the top priority for release. Whilst prisoners had escaped from the fortress before, most had been recaptured within hours and the underground Resistance did not want the same to happen to their valuable war hero.

It was easier to escape from the hospital where the prisoners were more lightly guarded than the main prison so it was decided to pretend that Whitney was desperately sick. Donald smuggled in a nasty-tasting drug which gave the patient stomach-ache and managed to pass it on to Whitney. Whitney swallowed it instantly and shortly after Donald had left, he began rolling around on the floor in agony and being sick. He wasn't fooling either – the effects were genuine. Whitney was put in the local hospital. His symptoms began to ease the following day and, dressed as a male nurse, he made his escape. Safely back in England, he sent Donald a coded message telling him that his escape had been successful, and inviting him to his home in England after the war.

The prison was in uproar after Whitney's escape and security measures were tightened. But Donald still thought himself safe enough and continued to bring files and forged papers tucked between the sheets of his hymn books.

One day, as Donald struggled with a large sack up to the gates of the prison, he was surprised by the loud honking of a goose. Turning round he saw a village lad chasing after the escaped bird. Donald dropped the sack and went to help, grasping the bird by its feet.

Taking the struggling goose out of the pastor's hands, the boy looked straight at Donald and instead of thanking him for his help warned him to keep walking. Donald returned for his sack and followed the boy.

'You are Monsieur le Canard?'

Donald was shaken and immediately suspicious. This was the nickname given to him by Pat O'Leary as a joke. Canard means 'duck' in French and Pat's pet name for the pastor was 'Donald Duck'.

'You must be careful today,' the boy warned, 'today they will search your sack.'

The boy turned on his heel and was off whilst Donald hurriedly looked for a safe place to stash all the forbidden goods. Near the roadside he found a sewer outlet pipe and, wrapping his contraband carefully, he hid it just above the pipe's exit.

The Search

Donald then returned to the path up to the gates of the prison, where he was met by two guards who greeted him with broad grins.

'The commandant of the prison wants to see you. Follow me!' they ordered.

Donald was shown into the office where a paunchy colonel, smoking the stub of a short cigar, greeted him. 'Ah, the man of God. I understand you bring "comfort" to the men,' he sneered. He strode up to Donald, his hands on his hips. 'Open the sack!' he ordered.

The contents were tipped on to the floor. The colonel was clearly expecting to find all sorts of unlawful goods but only innocent Bibles, hymn books and paperback books lay around his shiny black boots. He fell to his knees and immediately looked ridiculous as he scrambled amongst the papers searching for incriminating evidence.

Embarrassed and angry after his fruitless search, he sprang back to his feet. 'Sergeant! Get this man out of here!'

Donald could not resist a broad grin to himself as he joined the prisoners and conducted the service. As the men sang and the harmonium wailed out the hymns, Donald just had time to explain to the senior officer that the prison sewer pipe could provide a good means of escape. There they could pick up the forged identity papers that they needed.

A most ambitious plan was now hatched which would embarrass the Vichy government itself. Originally it was planned to help 150 prisoners escape but when news reached the Resistance from Britain that a waiting submarine could only accept 36, the plans were modified.

The entrance to the sewer was found and after a French worker was overpowered the men, in batches of six, entered the sewer pipe and crawled to freedom. One and a half hours later they were all safely out and making their way to the coast. All 36 made it back to England.

Some others who had not been chosen decided to chance their luck in solo escapes but were foiled when an overweight RAF squadron leader got wedged in the tunnel. They couldn't budge him and in the scuffle that took place to try and free him the alarm was raised and they were discovered.

Arrest

Once more, Donald had been under suspicion for months but the authorities had been unable to link him directly with the escapes. Eventually their patience snapped and evidence or not they were determined to put an end to his activities.

One late evening after Donald had been visiting Jewish friends, he made his way back to his boarding house. He tiptoed upstairs so as not to wake anyone and entered his room quietly, crossing the bedroom in darkness before switching on his bedside light. Before he could do so, however, the room light clicked behind him and he turned to face five revolvers all pointing in his direction.

'Pastor Donald Caskie, you are under arrest.'

Donald remained silent as handcuffs were locked around his wrists. They were too small and he winced as they cut into his flesh. It was May 1943 and Donald believed that the end of his life was near.

He was taken to the Villa Lynwood. In happier times before the war this had been the luxurious home of a rich English lady. Now, it was managed by the Italians, Gestapo collaborators, and it had become a place of torture and despair.

Donald was thrown into a filthy cell and, when the guards remembered, a hunk of hard bread and some water was thrust through the bars. A bucket for his toilet stood in the corner. The names of previous prisoners were etched into the crumbling plaster walls. God only knew what had become of them.

Donald was handed over to the Gestapo and eventually placed in the notorious prison of Fresnes, five miles south of Paris. On 22 November he heard jack boots approach his cell. The door was flung open.

'Pastor Donald Caskie. You are to be taken to court.'

In the corridor, he was handcuffed to another prisoner and thrown into the back of a police van. As they propped their backs against the van wall, the thin-faced Frenchman, trembling with fear, turned to Donald. 'I have been told I will die today.'

Donald suspected that he was to meet the same end himself. They talked and Donald tried to calm the young man down as he talked of his wife and children.

The van pulled to a halt and the young man was uncuffed from Donald.

'Not you!' a soldier commanded, pointing to Donald. The pastor jumped down from the back of the van and asked the guard if he could have two minutes with the Frenchman. His request was granted. The pastor spoke of the war that would soon come to an end and told him to take some comfort in the fact that his wife and children would be safe. The tears streamed down the man's face as Donald said his farewells and climbed back into the van.

Donald was taken to a courtroom where after a brief trial he was sentenced to death. Whilst he waited for the death sentence to be carried out he asked to see a German pastor. He didn't expect the request to be met and was surprised when it was granted.

The meeting proved to be the saving of Donald Caskie. As they talked, they realized as pastors they had many friends in common. Hans Peters left Donald's cell and pleaded for his life, arguing that the evidence against Donald was almost entirely based on the unreliable evidence of a double agent. On 7 January 1944 his death sentence was lifted but it was not until August, when the Allies entered Paris, that the prisoners of the Gestapo at Fresnes were released from their cells.

Justice

Shortly after his release Donald returned to his beloved Scottish church in the Rue Bayard, Paris, and attempted to pick up his ministry once more. So many people had disappeared. Everyone's lives had been disrupted. He wondered what fate had befallen his comrades in the underground. So many of them had been betrayed by the Gestapo agent Cole.

He was delighted to learn that Pat O'Leary had survived. He brought news with him when he came to see Donald.

'Cole? Dead and good riddance,' he explained. 'We found out where he was hiding. Half a dozen men went after him, knocked his door down. He tried to resist but was shot and killed in the gun battle that followed.'

Honouring the Tartan Pimpernel

Donald returned to his duties as the minister of the Scottish church in Paris and was awarded the OBE and the French OCF. In 1961 he returned to Scotland where

Dr Caskie looks at the foundation stone of the new Scottish Church in Paris, 1957.

he serves a minister until 1968. Pastor Donald Caskie, nicknamed the 'Tartan Pimpernel' for helping so many prisoners of war to escape, died on 27 December 1983.

FIGHTING FACTS

Ways of Resisting

There were many ways in which the Resistance movements throughout Europe helped the Allies.

Intelligence – passing on information about the enemy. Often women and children were best suited to this kind of work as the Germans suspected them less. Information was vital if the Allies were about to launch an attack.

Subversion – all sorts of methods were used to damage the enemy. Vital bridges and railway lines were blown up and false stories were spread to fool them.

Rescuing prisoners of war or preventing them from being captured. This was the main work of Dr Caskie. Not only were soldiers and airmen needed to continue the fight back home but they often knew vital pieces of information which would help the Intelligence Services.

A Daring Raid

One French Resistance group employed a stonemason to cut through a wall to where the Germans were storing petrol. Driving a tanker up to the wall, they ran a pipe through the wall and siphoned out the petrol. The mason then rebuilt the wall. Returning the next night, they pumped out more petrol and, knowing the Germans would realize supplies were going down, they poured sugar into the remaining tanks.

Resistance Armies

In the former Yugoslavia, the Resistance general Marshall Tito built up an army of 250,000. Towards the end of the war in France the French Resistance army, the Maquis, struck against the Germans to draw off forces that would have been sent against the Allied invasion.

There were also resistance movements in Germany itself. One group nearly succeeded in blowing up Hitler himself on 20 July 1944. If caught, resistance fighters everywhere could expect to suffer torture and execution.

THE CITY THAT REFUSED TO DIE

BATTLE BRIEFING

Throughout the late summer of 1940 London suffered the full onslaught of the German bombing campaign. But during October, the tactics changed and the weight of the **Luftwaffe***'s attack shifted to target industrial cities in the north.*

Herman Goering, commander of the Luftwaffe, boasted to the Führer that his bombers alone could bring Britain to its knees by destroying Britain's armaments industry. And to prove his point, one city in the north of England was chosen for a devastating attack. Under the code name 'Moonlight Sonata', the whole of the long-range German bomber force was aimed at the heart of one city — Coventry — an important industrial base in the Midlands.

Since the attacks would be at night, German scientists had invented a method to guide the bombers to their target using

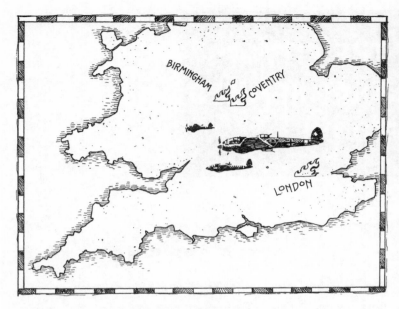

Some of the cities hit by bombing raids.

radio waves. This worked by transmitting radio signals from two radio stations far apart from one another. By aiming the beams at a city in Britain they could guide the bombers to the point where the signals crossed.

In June 1940, however, the British had learnt of this invention and prevented the Germans using it. By sending radio signals of their own they were able to jam or deflect the German signals. This proved very effective. One officer's wife evacuated to the countryside wrote to her husband that she was astonished to see hundreds of bombs dropped on empty fields, miles from any town.

The Germans improved their system. Guided by a different type of radio signal, German pathfinder aircraft flew to the dropping zone ahead of the bombers. Once the target area had been identified, it was lit up with thousands of 'fire-bombs', called 'incendiaries'.

British scientists nearly found a way to jam these signals too but unfortunately one scientist made a mistake when working out the calculation. This mistake was to cost the people of Coventry dear.

At 19:00 on 14 November, the first German bombers crossed the target area and began to release incendiaries. The raiders first set fire to the ancient medieval centre, reducing the cathedral to a smoking ruin. Wave after wave of bombers poured bombs into the city in an attack which lasted over ten hours.

As the grey light of morning broke on the 15th, one third of the city's houses had been destroyed, all telephones were out of action and no trains or buses ran. One hundred acres of the city centre had been totally destroyed. The casualty list was terrible – 554 men, women and children had been killed and over 1,200 were seriously injured.

Nazi propaganda went into top gear. The Germans were convinced they had delivered a deathblow to the city. No one, they were sure, could have lived through the horror of that night, no factory could have been left standing. They even believed a new word was necessary to describe destruction on this scale – 'Coventration'.

But they were wrong. The city slowly revived. The next morning, people stumbled through the remains of fallen walls and shattered windows to the shops, offices and factories where they worked. Within five weeks they were back to full production.

And yet the Germans had almost succeeded in killing the city, for all the water supplies had been knocked out. Had they followed up their raid the next night, the fires started would have been out of control.

Coventry's sufferings did not end on that terrible night. At the darkest moment of the war, a further terrible raid followed on 8 April 1941 but again, with grim determination, Coventry stirred into life afterwards.

And so the city lived on. And it lived on because ordinary people, who never dreamed that they were the stuff of heroes, found within themselves the courage to think of others. One of them was Edna Viner, seventeen years old and just beginning her nursing career.

Date: 14 November 1940
Place: Coventry

A Moonlit Night

'At last – a whole evening to myself.' Probationary nurse Edna Viner studied her reflection in the bus window. A gentle smile spread across her face. She loved her job even though the hours were numbingly long. From seven in the morning until nine at night, she scurried about the corridors and wards of the Coventry and Warwickshire hospital, always at the beck and call of other nurses and the dreaded matron. And if she paused for breath, she would be spurred into activity with the all-too familiar cry, 'Nurse Viner! Don't you know there's a war on?' Yes, like everyone else she was only too aware that there was a war on – food was scarce and rationed, towns and cities cloaked in blackout.

But when her smile lit up patients' faces and children in pain found comfort in her touch then she knew why she had chosen to be a nurse.

'Yes, that's what makes the hours melt away,' she thought. Blinking her eyes, she looked beyond her own reflection to the silhouettes of the city as they sped by. Bathed in the strange silvery sheen of a full moon it felt like a city of ghosts. Windows were blacked out so that no chink of light escaped. Car and bus headlights were masked except for a slit of rectangular light that pierced the gloom. Street lamps were reduced to no more than tiny pinpricks of light.

To thread one's way through the streets under such conditions was filled with danger. Road accidents had doubled in the first year of the war. People broke legs falling down dimly lit steps or stumbling over the edge of railway platforms, or drowned by accidentally walking into canals.

In 1940 the government had decided it might be safer for its citizens if the regulations were relaxed. For the first time since the beginning of the war, people were allowed to use hand torches as long as they were covered with a double layer of tissue paper. Other ideas had their comical side. Men left their white shirt-tails hanging outside their trousers so they could be seen in the dark. And to improve eyesight in the dark, the Ministry of Information encouraged everyone to eat more carrots, for it was a 'well-known fact' that night bomber pilots owed the accuracy of their bombing to munching their way through platefuls of this humble vegetable.

Black Snow

As Edna relaxed in the dim glow of the bus interior, she felt safe and secure. She took some comfort from the fact that there had been few bombing raids on Coventry, just the occasional stray. 'Not like London,' she thought. 'Those poor people had suffered night after night because of Herman Goering who boasted London would fall and with it, the rest of the country. Well, he'd been wrong about the Battle of Britain. Our pilots had shown him. The same will be true of London and the people of Coventry, if it comes to that.'

For such a gentle girl, Edna had a streak of determination running through her, which would not allow her to be bullied. She clenched her lips together and jutted her chin out firmly in defiance. And then she giggled at herself. She'd just caught sight of her own reflection in the bus window.

'All the same, everyone says that Jerry'll never find Coventry,' advised the older generation.

Edna mulled this pearl of wisdom over in her mind as she nestled into the seat. 'All the older people of the

City say we're safe 'cos Coventry's in a hollow,' she thought. They'd explained this to Edna by making a cup shape with their hands. 'We're right at the bottom and can't be reached, you see!' This gave a measure of comfort to everyone, for people were keen to believe that it was really true.

But they were terribly wrong.

This particular night the moon was full and there was not a cloud in the sky. It was so bright, in fact, that you could read a newspaper without any artificial light. 'It's so beautiful,' thought Edna, for everywhere was bathed in a glowing silver light. For years to come the mere sight of a full moon would remind her of that terrifying night of death and destruction.

Edna craned her neck to look up at the moon. It seemed unnaturally bright – glowing like an incandescent flare. And then she noticed that the eerie silvery light was not mere moonlight. Thousands upon thousands of pathfinder chandelier flares were falling on the city. It would have been beautiful if they had not had such a deadly purpose.

Moments later, incendiary bombs began to burst in orange flashes. Within seconds flickering tongues of flames licked up the sides of buildings, bursting windows to the tinkling sound of falling glass. The air-raid siren whined its warning as people stared at the sky then hurried for the shelters. Powerful searchlights sent pillars of light hundreds of feet into the air, stabbing at the darkness, searching for the enemy overhead. The bark of anti-aircraft guns added to the maddening sounds of explosions as they spat out 130 2 lb rounds every minute.

It took Edna only seconds to reach her decision. There would be casualties and she would be needed. Pushing her way to the boarding platform at the back of the bus, Edna grasped the pole to steady herself and then dropped down to the road. Sprinting down the street, she hammered on the door of the friend's house she had just left.

'What the—' Edna's friend was surprised to see her but immediately understood why she had returned. As they slammed the door behind them, the whole terrace shook as the first high explosive bombs landed.

Proud Victorian buildings swayed and fell crashing to the ground in a shower of dust and flame. Meanwhile, the heart of the city was taking a severe pounding. The medieval cathedral, which had stood for centuries, was hit by incendiaries and high explosive bombs. The spire trembled and fell. Blackened oak beams crackled and burst into flames.

Edna and her friend clambered into the cupboard beneath the stairs and held on to one another as the whole house shook with the repeated blasts of exploding bombs. Edna wanted to get back to the hospital as soon as possible but realized that this was out of the question for the time being.

Muffled sounds of hammering managed to reach them

despite the mayhem that was taking place outside. Someone was thumping on the front door. They raced to open it, flinging the door wide open. The street had been turned into a vision of hell. Neighbours were dragging bedding. Children were howling, clutching hold of their parents' hands as they were dragged to safety in the public shelters. A dog shot past their door, maddened by the noise.

Hertford Street, Coventry, after the bombing.

'Get to the shelters – NOW!" The air-raid warden barked out his order as he dashed to the next house and thumped on their neighbour's door. Half the street was ablaze. Dense acrid smoke billowed out from buildings, burning their nostrils and choking their throats, whilst soot danced and swirled like black snow, fluttering in the heat.

Cauldron of Fire

Several thousand feet up, Oberleutnant Manfred Deschner, bomber pilot in the main attack force, peered out of the cockpit window at the sea of flames that had once been Coventry. The trip had been easy. Steering by means of radio signals, the bombers had been kept on course by dots and dashes crackling over their earphones. But this had soon proved unnecessary, for the crimson glow of fires feeding on fires could be seen soon after they crossed the English coast.

Some pilots thought of the mothers and children perishing in the narrow terraced streets below. 'But,' they thought, 'these stubborn Englanders only have themselves to blame. If only they had surrendered after the fall of France there would be no need for this slaughter. Even now it might not be too late to realize that resistance against Germany under the Führer is foolish, and a quick end to the bloodshed could be found if they come to their senses.'

Patients First

Edna was determined to return to the hospital but until

A car in a bomb crater.

there was a pause in the bombing she couldn't leave the shelter. And she would certainly be needed, for as soon as the first bombs began to fall, yellow alert had been sounded for all nurses to move to action stations.

One of the first in the hospital to heed the call was

Sister Emma Horne, a stout, no-nonsense nurse. At the sound of the alarm, she brushed her already starched uniform down, pushed her glasses up the bridge of her nose and went into action.

At the other end of the hospital, Matron Joyce Burton gave herself one last look in the mirror and walked to the wards. 'Matrons,' she told herself, 'must set a good example. They must remain calm and confident. THEY DO NOT RUN!'

All around the hospital grounds incendiary bombs spluttered into life, whilst the hospital staff ran from one to the other trying to douse them with buckets of sand. But their task was huge. No sooner had one been extinguished than another burst into life. Fires were springing up all around and the nurses' home was well alight. They were quickly evacuated to the main building – and just in the nick of time. As the last nurse made her escape, a high explosive bomb crashed through the concrete floor and demolished it.

Inside the main building, the nurses quietly and purposefully paced the wards, calming patients and preparing others for evacuation to the ground floor and basement. There they were made as comfortable as possible under beds covered with mattresses.

While this was happening incendiaries and high explosive bombs were raining down on the battered city. But the danger did not deter doctors and nurses from ferrying their patients from some of the outlying buildings to the relative safety of the main building. Sister Horne and Matron Burton led the way. Nurses and doctors gave no thought to their own safety. Red-hot shrapnel buzzed around the quadrangle, whilst deadly blades of shattered glass slashed and pierced whoever they came into contact with. Patients, aware of the sacrifice that was being made for their safety, did not make a murmur, despite the jolting they received as they were carried along on stretchers.

The unusual circumstances demanded unusual methods. Doctors even pulled patients on to their own backs to transport them quickly. No sooner had the last patient been delivered to the main building than a high explosive bomb ripped through the men's ward and destroyed it completely.

Inferno

Edna crouched in the shelter, squeezing the hands of nearby children every time they jumped at the detonation of a bomb. Above their concrete home the town was burning, for the fire service was rapidly running out of water supplies to quench the flames. The nearby canal, from which the fire service had been drawing most of their water, had been breached. Water hydrants were buried under tons of fallen masonry and the firemen could do nothing but gaze helplessly as the inferno engulfed the city.

Gas mains began to blow in violent fountains of flames. Electricity cables fizzled and went dead. The hospital was particularly badly hit as the power supplies began to fail. Hospital generators deep in the basement whirred into action but after a few minutes spluttered and died. Nurses and doctors were forced to work by the dim glare of hurricane lamps, ironically stamped with the phrase 'Made in Germany'.

Inevitably, firemen were amongst the first casualties. Many were suffering wounds from fragments of hot metal from bursting bombs. Their faces were greasy and black with oily smoke and streaked with tears and sweat. They gripped the sides of chairs, trying not to call out in pain as nurses and doctors probed their skin for shards of metal. As soon as they were stitched up, they were on their feet and making their way back to the worst of the fires.

At two o'clock in the morning the noise of battle began to subside as, one by one, the anti-aircraft guns fell into silence. Not that the raid was over. Far from it. The truth was that the barrels of the guns had become so hot they were no longer capable of firing. And the raid continued. For hour after devastating hour.

In the Light of Morning

As the grey light of morning began to break the bombers turned and headed back for the airfields on mainland Europe. They had fired 6,700 rounds but not one of them, out of 449, had been brought down.

They left a city smouldering and in ruins. Deep in the shelters, people stared at the ceiling with red-rimmed eyes, ears pricked to catch the slightest sound. 'Had they gone? HAD THEY REALLY GONE?' they wondered. After ten hours of constant bombardment the silence was welcome but unreal.

'All clear. It's all over.' The air-raid warden's voice seeped into the underground shelters and people slowly emerged, blinking in the early morning light. A fine drizzly rain settled in beads on their clothing as they stared about the smouldering and shattered landscape, trying to find a landmark amongst the ruins that they could recognize. Glass crunched beneath tired feet as they massaged their stiff and aching limbs back into life. Scattered amongst the ruins, scraps of clothes mingled with sewing machines, twisted bicycle wheels, a child's doll and the bodies of the dead.

Edna decided she must pick her way through the ruined streets and get to the hospital as fast as she could. This was not easy, for in addition to the mountains of rubble many areas were cordoned off where unexploded bombs had been discovered.

When Edna finally arrived at the hospital her mouth dropped open in horror. Every window had been blown in, doors had been blasted from their hinges and there were great gaping holes in the walls.

The nurses' home was completely gutted. Patients with multiple fractures who could not be moved had cracked jokes as they had watched through a hole blasted in the roof of the hospital bombers high above caught in the glare of the searchlights. Surgeons had carried on operating throughout, occasionally diving beneath the operating table when a bomb exploded close by.

Dr Winter, one of the surgeons, recalled, 'Throughout the packed hospital there was not one cry of fear, not a sign of panic.' They'd simply got on with the job of helping others.

Amazingly, only one person was killed in the hospital. A soldier on leave had rushed into the hospital to help rescue patients and had sadly become the victim of a direct hit.

Edna Viner was proud to have such colleagues, proud to count herself among such heroes. Not that they thought of themselves as such. They were simply doing what they had been trained to do – to take care of patients.

The ordeal was not over, however. No sooner had they began clearing up when the air-raid wardens sounded the alarm. A delayed-action bomb had just been discovered next to the operating theatre. Orders came for the whole hospital to be evacuated because there might be others.

Edna now had a chance to play her part. In less than an hour all the patients were safely on their way to neighbouring hospitals. Edna had begun her nursing career in the most difficult of circumstances but had, like those around her, risen to the challenge.

The ruins of Coventry Cathedral.

FIGHTING FACTS

Breaking the Code

Prime Minister Churchill knew that Coventry was the sole target for attack that night. Three days earlier, the secret code-breaking headquarters at Bletchley had discovered a German signal which described a massive air-attack, code-named 'Moonlight Sonata'. The Germans used the code 'umbrella' for the city that was to suffer the raid and at first British Intelligence thought this referred to Birmingham. Neville Chamberlain, the prime minister before Churchill, had often been photographed carrying a rolled umbrella, and he came from Birmingham.

Soon after, another piece of information came to light that indicated the raid would be on Coventry. Why this information was never used to warn the people of Coventry is something of a mystery. Perhaps the government was afraid that people would panic and this would cause even more injury, or they may have wanted to protect the fact that they had broken the German secret code.

Whatever the reason, it was not until 15:00 hours on 14 November that RAF Fighter Command was told of the impending attack.

Death of Chamberlain

Neville Chamberlain, the prime minister at the outbreak of war, had done everything he could to avoid war.

Unfortunately, he had taken Hitler at his word when the dictator declared that Germany did not want to conquer countries in Europe. Chamberlain gave in to Hitler's demands and this only encouraged the Führer to demand more.

Ill with cancer and broken in spirit, Chamberlain gave way to Churchill, who became Prime Minister and vowed Britain would fight Germany on the beaches and on the streets. Neville Chamberlain died on the night of 14 November, the very same night that Germany launched its devastating raid on Coventry.

Land Mine Horror

The Germans also dropped massive land mines, which were timed to explode after the air raid, when it was assumed it would be all clear. They could blow up a whole square mile of buildings.

On the night of the Coventry raid one of these coffin-shaped canisters was mistaken for a supply box. Several Home Guard volunteers shot at it but fortunately missed. When it landed, several more volunteers dragged it to one side before someone recognized it and ordered them to leave it for the bomb disposal squad.

Bomb Shelters

Sir John Anderson, the Home Secretary before the war, ordered the mass production of cheap air-raid shelters which, because he had introduced them, became known as Anderson Shelters. Nearly one and a half million had been given away free by September 1939. Each could hold six adults. There were problems with them from the start, however. They frequently became waterlogged and you needed a garden to put them in. Fewer than one in four people had one so the government came up with

Inside an Anderson Shelter.

an indoor version – the Morrison Shelter, named after the government minister Herbert Morrison. This was little more than a steel-mesh box with a mattress inside. It could hold two adults and two children, and people often stored it under their dining table. Over a million Morrison shelters were issued.

Women at Work

Women had played an important part in World War I when they had released many men for front-line duties by taking over their jobs. They played an even bigger part in World War II. Factory work and life in the services offered great opportunities for independence. Those women registered with the Ministry of Labour, however, had no choice and they could be directed to the services or to war work, as the Ministry decided.

This did not mean that men and women were treated as equals though. Men still earned better wages even when the women took over their jobs in the factories. Those women who joined the services probably gained the most. They learned skills that had once been for men and travelled to places they might not otherwise have gone. After the war, they were expected to give up their jobs to men returning home.

Many women also gave up their time voluntarily to help the war effort. The Women's Volunteer Service was one such organization.

The Home Guard

On 14 May 1941 at the height of the battle for France a radio appeal was made for volunteers to join a new group called the Local Defence Volunteers – the LDV. Their job was to defend Britain if any Germans landed. By August, the LDV had nearly one and a half million volunteers. It was a part-time force and unpaid. At first there were no uniforms so they wore armbands instead. There were few weapons and so many carried out drill using broom shanks, and one northern branch actually drilled with spears loaned by a retired colonel.

Later they were given proper training, uniforms and rifles and renamed the Home Guard. But they were better known as 'Dad's Army' because of the age of the volunteers, many of whom were World War 1 veterans. Their job was to defend factories, shipyards and munitions works in their own area and to assist in air-raid precautions. By late 1944 it was clear that the feared invasion would now never happen and Dad's Army was disbanded.

WAR OF
THE JUST

BATTLE BRIEFING

*The Nazis believed that they were a superior race and perse-
cuted members of other races they thought inferior, particularly Jewish people.*

*As soon as Hitler took power in 1933 he began to pass
laws. Jews were banned from being teachers, lawyers and
doctors, and from working in the government. On the streets
his bully-boys organized demonstrations against Jewish busi-
nesses and shops.*

*In 1935, no Jew was allowed to be a German citizen and
they were forbidden to marry non-Jews. They were turned
down for jobs and many shopkeepers refused to serve them.*

*In November 1938 a young Jew killed a German official
living in Paris. Nazi mobs took to the streets and attacked
Jews in revenge. They killed 91 Jews and many synagogues
were burned to the ground. They also rounded up 20,000*

A Jewish synagogue in Berlin, after being
set on fire by the mob.

Jews and took them to camps. This night was known as
'Kristallnacht' because of the broken glass that covered the
streets afterwards.

Many Jewish people decided to leave the country as soon

as they could and fled to France, Britain and the United States of America. These were the lucky ones, for when war broke out in 1939, Hitler gave orders for all Jews to be arrested and put into camps.

With the Nazi conquest of Europe, millions more Jews came under Nazi control. Many were shot or forced to live in tiny walled areas of cities called ghettos where they died of starvation and disease. Finally, they were herded into death camps where they were killed.

Some Germans tried to help the Jews whilst some Jews took up arms against the Nazis.

This is the harrowing story of one survivor saved by ten Allied prisoners of war.

Date: January 1945
Place: Village of Gross Golemkau, Poland

Sam's War

Sam Wells stared out over the bleak, icy fields of the Polish village of Gross Golemkau, near to the border with Germany. It was January 1945 and he hoped the war would soon be over. True, the Allied advance had stalled because the Germans put up a bitter fight but slowly they were being pushed back into Germany and whether it took another year or so the Germans would eventually lose. It was all a matter of time.

And, in the meantime, Sam had to cling on to life. He'd managed for five years all right, ever since his capture at Dunkirk in 1940. He'd been one of the unlucky ones

The village of Gross Golemkau, Poland.

ordered to stay behind and fight a rearguard action whilst the remnants of the British Expeditionary Force clambered aboard just about anything that floated and made it back to Blighty. Well, somebody had to do it. In some ways he hadn't minded, for it had meant that Britain was still able to continue the fight when all hope seemed lost.

But on the other hand, it had been five years, five long years. He'd got over the humiliation of being marched through Holland, the country they'd come to protect, filing past those sullen Dutch faces that presented a mixture of despair and pity for the British 'tommies'.

Some had even risked a beating for passing bread to the soldiers as they marched into captivity. German soldiers, whose faces were full of the joy and arrogance of victory, had herded them along. Well, the tables had been turned. Germany was clinging on to fragments of Holland, desperately trying to stop the Allied armies crossing into Germany and bringing the thousand-year Reich crashing down in the rubble of Berlin.

But a side that is losing can lash out and cause destruction. And the German army had shown no mercy in its retreat from Russia. In the east the war was fought without rules. Whole villages were massacred, without regard as to whether the innocent victims were women or children. Sam had seen some of the horrors for himself and heard the stories of the terrified refugees fleeing from the Red (Russian) Army – stiffened corpses by the roadside, villages ablaze, animals slaughtered. And as the Russian army advanced, they too were showing no mercy to those whom they suspected of helping the Germans and as they neared Germany itself they were craving revenge.

To stay alive, that occupied everybody's mind. Sam had been set to work on a farm and this had helped him survive, for whilst those in towns starved, at least there was always the chance of something to eat in the countryside. Even this advantage, however, was fast disappearing and all that was left was a few root crops normally left for the animals. Snow covered the ground.

Sam wrapped himself tighter in his army greatcoat, glancing at his painfully thin frame. 'They could fit two of me in here now,' he thought. 'My own ma wouldn't recognize me.' Sam was lean and sinewy when he joined the army, but now he seemed to be just lean, for his muscles were beginning to waste to flabby pouches of skin.

'But just think of the money the army owes me now. Five years' pay. I'll be the richest bloke in the street. With all that cash . . . why, I should be able to afford a . . . bicycle.' He even managed to raise a smile at this thought, for nobody got rich on army pay.

Sam toed a mound of dirt with his boot, which was patched with cardboard, when he was jolted from his thoughts by the sound of a German guard barking out an order to hurry.

An Army of Ghosts

'Schnell! Schnell!'

Sam jumped to his feet, thinking the order was directed at him. He'd been so preoccupied with his own thoughts that he'd not noticed a most sorrowful procession enter the village. What surprised Sam most was the fact that they were all women, but now they resembled the most distressing army of skeletons. They came straggling through the bitter cold, about 300 of them, on the point of collapse. Starved as their bodies clearly were, even their slight weight seemed too much for them to carry. Some helped to support one another but in the freezing snow they lost their footing and slipped to the ground, only to be forced on to their feet again by the guards.

The icy wind whipped through their thin rayon dresses, for most had no coats. Their faces were chalk-like, drained of blood, their lips pinched and blue as ice, their hair filthy and matted. They stared at the villagers, holding out dishevelled hands in a plea for a scrap of bread or a winter cabbage leaf.

This band of women were all that were left of 1,200 Jewish women who had been force-marched from the Stutthof death camp, deep in Lithuania. The Russian army was now in control of the camp and the Germans had retreated, taking their prisoners with them. They'd walked all day and slept at night in any barn the SS guards could find – often packed so tightly that they had to take turns to sleep huddled on the ground. In the 200-kilometre, six-week march, 900 had died. Those that couldn't walk were shot. Some died from hunger, others from the cold.

At the time the Allies didn't know of the existence of the death camps. Only the odd rumour had leaked to the outside world. But it was as obvious to Sam as to the rest of the crowd who gathered to watch that these people had been brutally treated.

As Sam watched them file past he noticed one girl lift her head and stare into his face. She could have been no more than sixteen or seventeen, although her body and face were so wasted that she could have been thirty or even forty. Starvation had already etched lines deep into her face. Her cheeks were hollowed and her dark eyes were so deep within her pale face that Sam gained the distinct impression he was staring at a skull.

The image of that face stayed with Sam long after the line of women and their guards had passed. The snow had turned to a slushy yellow with the tramp of their feet but as they disappeared into the distance fresh flurries of snow fell like feathers and began to cover their tracks.

The scattered groups of villagers who had been watching them file past turned and melted back into the village. Some now regretted that they'd put their trust in Hitler, for their comfortable world was now falling apart and they could expect no mercy from the advancing Russian army. Some tried to ease their consciences by saying they had never wanted things to go this far – not to death marches. If only the Jews had not been so rich, if only they'd behaved more like Germans, they argued to themselves. Most forgot that, as German-speaking people in Poland, they'd cheered when the German army advanced in 1939. Then they'd been proud of being part of Hitler's Greater German Reich.

Rescue

Sam pulled himself up into the driving seat of the horse-drawn cart. It was piled high with turnips, which he'd been ordered to take to the barn at the end of the village for storage. He slapped the reins on to the horses' backs and followed the ragged army of survivors. A heavy curtain of snowflakes swirled and danced but he kept the pitiful procession in view.

They passed the barn where he was meant to deliver the turnips but although the horses attempted to stop Sam moved them on. He could not explain why he was doing this but he felt drawn to follow the procession ahead. Above all, he could not erase the girl's face from his mind.

A short distance beyond Sam's supposed destination, the lead guard unslung his rifle and ordered a halt. The other guards moved down the line, counting the prisoners, before they herded them into a ramshackle barn with half its roof missing. As the guards moved back up the line, Sam noticed one of the ragged shadows slink to the edge of the road and roll into the ditch. She began to haul herself along on her elbows in Sam's direction and although wet patches of snow clung to her back she was still highly visible in the black rags she was wearing.

The rear guards, who'd counted and reported the number of prisoners to the officer in charge at the head of the column, now turned and began to march back down the line. They'd almost certainly catch the movement of their prisoner as she slithered along the ditch, for the road sloped back down to the village and she would be spotted.

'Giddy up!' Sam clicked the horses into a trot. He knew he must try and distract the German guards. If they focused on him they might not notice the girl worming her way back along the ditch. He couldn't stand by and see her shot.

Sam made as much noise as he could goading the horses along the track. At first the two guards were startled and unslung their rifles, but when they saw the cause of the commotion, they used the butts of their rifles to jab the survivors into the barn.

Sam pulled the cart to a halt as soon as he was alongside the girl and, turning his head towards her whilst keeping his eyes fixed on the guards up ahead, indicated with a nod of his head for her to stay where she was for the time being. He dismounted and ran his hand along the back of the left-hand horse, then he crouched as if he was examining its hoof for a stone. This gave him the chance to look back to the village and make sure they were not being watched. He left the horse and went back to the cart, this time crouching by the wheel. He'd picked up a fair amount of the German language whilst a prisoner of war and in his poor German ordered the girl to keep low and slide under the cart. This she did and as she looked up into Sam's face he saw at once it was the face of the girl that had so haunted him.

A Close Shave

'Don't be afraid. I'm going to hide you in a barn. They'll check again and find you missing. We've got to make sure you are tucked away safe.'

The girl looked into Sam's face. He looked honest but war changes everything. 'Are you Polish?' she asked.

'No, I'm British,' Sam replied, and when the girl looked puzzled he explained that he was a prisoner of war.

She was in a terrible state – worn out and frighteningly thin. At this sudden act of kindness the tears streamed down her face.

'Enough, girl. You'll get us caught.' He took her by the arm and after a few nervous glances around bundled her on to the back of the cart and hid her beneath a pile of turnips.

'Now, take this.' Sam gave her a hunk of bread, which she wolfed down. They reached the barn and Sam unloaded the turnips, explaining that he lived with nine other British prisoners of war in a makeshift gaol. Each day they went to work for different farmers in the area but they were allowed a considerable degree of freedom to come and go as they pleased. The girl told him her name was Sara.

'Now, you must stay in hiding here. I'll be back with help. The farmer's wife comes in here at night to check the cows so you'll have to keep well out of sight.' Sam patted Sara's head and told her not to worry. Before leaving he hid the lantern in the hope that the farmer's wife would only have a quick look in the barn to make sure everything was all right. He then left to report back to the guard.

Sara climbed into the feeding trough and covered herself with straw for warmth. Her mind raced. Could she trust this Britisher? If she were caught the guards would shoot her on the spot.

Around midnight, Sara heard the creak of the barn door as it opened. She closed her eyes tightly, determined not to move a muscle.

'Where's that cursed lantern? It was here this morning.'

Sara heard the rustle of straw as the farmer's wife groped in the darkness for the lantern. Something metallic crashed to the floor, followed by the farmer's wife cursing. She could hear scratching as the woman tried to feel her way through the inky blackness towards where the cows were tethered. She was getting closer. Sara could hear the woman breathing and went even more rigid. The farmer's wife was at the trough. In seconds she would be discovered. The woman's fingers were inching towards her like a spider.

But Sara did not budge. 'What will be, will be. I can run no longer,' she said to herself.

Then the farmer's wife touched Sara's leg. But still the girl did not move.

'Who's there?' the farmer's wife called. 'Who's there?' She took hold of Sara's leg and shook it but Sara remained motionless.

The farmer's wife left her and groped her way back to the door and left. Would she raise the alarm? Would German guards come running to the scene? Sara decided that it was too dangerous to leave the barn. If she were not caught she would freeze to death — it was better to stay where she was.

She slept little that night, expecting a posse of German soldiers to come crashing and shouting into the barn. This did not happen and she could not understand why.

Success!

'Good morning,' Sam greeted the farmer's wife. She and her husband had been fairly decent to the prisoners of war, particularly as news filtered through that the Russians were fast approaching.

'A strange thing happened last night,' she replied. 'I was checking the barn where you stored the turnips yesterday. I couldn't find the lantern and had to grope my way in to check the cows.'

Sam's heart sank. Had Sara been discovered?

She continued, 'I knew someone was there and I was a little scared but they kept so still I reckoned they were more frightened of me. I'm sure it was an army deserter. Who can blame them? The war's over!'

She suddenly remembered that someone else might be listening and nervously turned around to check. Defeatist talk such as this could mean the death sentence so everyone had to keep up the big lie that Hitler was luring the Allied armies into Germany before he turned on them and wiped them out. Nobody believed it but no one dared speak out.

'Anyway they've gone. I had a look this morning.'

Saving Sara

Sam wondered what could have happened to Sara. There'd been fresh falls of snow during the night, which had rapidly turned to ice. If she weren't caught, she'd surely freeze to death. Even if she was still there he didn't have much good news to tell her. He'd been to the Russian women's camp a couple of miles outside the village but they'd told him they could not take the Jewish girl in, for if she was discovered the German guards would execute a number of them, innocent or guilty. So he'd gone back to his mates and asked them if they would take her in. They knew the penalties would be harsh if the German authorities found out. Not one of his comrades hesitated. If they could fool the Germans then that was a victory worth fighting for.

But was she still there?

'I'll go and have a look round,' said Sam.

Entering the barn, he whispered the girl's name above the lowing of the cattle. 'Sara, it's me, the British soldier. Are you there?'

The mound of turnips began to move and from their midst Sara's ashen face appeared.

'I know what happened last night. Don't worry, she won't be back. Meanwhile, we've got to get you out of here. I'm sending a mate down to collect you. You'll have to share our digs.'

Sam's mate, Willie Fisher, arrived about an hour

later, carrying a greatcoat and cap hidden under a sheet of canvas. Sara was a little afraid of him at first. Willie had a stammer and he slurred his words so badly that she thought he was drunk. Eventually, he gained her confidence and persuaded her to put the army coat on.

'We're gonna make a s-s-s-soldier of you!' He looked at her pathetically thin frame wrapped in the coat and the cap perched on the top of her matted hair. He instructed her how to march and salute until they were ready to face the world outside.

'Now look straight ahead when we leave and don't stop for anything,' ordered Willie. Sara nodded. Willie threw open the barn door as Sara blinked at the blinding snow outside.

'Right. One, two, three! One, two, three!' Willie barked out the commands as they marched towards the village. The villagers barely turned their heads, they were so used to seeing British prisoners of war working at the nearby farms. But would the German guards be so easily fooled?

Many of the guards were older men who had been excused active service and instead had been assigned to routine duties such as this. Few of them were dedicated Nazis, who tended to be younger.

Sara stumbled along and tried as best as she could to stay in step with Willie. But she was so weak and thin that she could hardly keep up with him.

119

So far so good, but the real test was just up ahead where Wilhelm Kuntz, the barrack guard, stamped his feet and blew into his gloved hands to keep warm. Willie kept Sara on his far side so she would be partially shielded. Willie got on well with Wilhelm. They both had the same name and the guard was not above smuggling a few treats to the men. He often referred to Hitler with contempt as 'the little corporal' because of the rank the German dictator had had in World War I.

Willie held up his hand in greeting as Wilhelm acknowledged him with a 'Ja'. In so doing he loosened his hold on Sara. The cuffs of her greatcoat, which had been tucked inside the sleeves, tumbled out and her hands disappeared from view.

Wilhelm sniggered. 'Girlfriend? That's good.'

Willie nodded back and smiled. That was too narrow an escape and he could feel the sweat prickle the back of his neck despite the cold weather.

Willie quickly got Sara inside the men's quarters. All ten lived in a single room, which was part of a stable block that was locked each night. Once the men were secured inside the hut the guards went down to their warm billets in the village.

A Family of Soldiers

'Come over here, you wee thing.' Tommy Noble was a Scottish soldier and instantly wanted to protect and help Sara. He'd already prepared a thin soup made from milk and vegetables but she had great difficulty in keeping the food in her stomach, for she'd had nothing decent to eat for months.

Alan Edwards and George Hammond dipped some cloths in paraffin and began to clean the lice from her hair. Bert Hamling was the medic amongst them and he began to rub a red ointment into the sores which covered her legs. She was in a terrible condition and only weighed about five stone.

After Sara had been cleaned up and fed, the prisoners hid her in the hayloft above the stables next to the chimney, where there was a false wall, to keep her warm. Each day they took food from their plates at the farms where they worked and smuggled it back to the stable block. Best of all was the arrival of the Red Cross parcels from Switzerland. Every prisoner of war was allowed to receive one although they often got delayed or were never seen again as the Germans helped themselves to the contents. The ones that got through contained precious tea, sugar and tins of meat. Sometimes they gave some of the food to the guards to bribe them.

Sara gradually recovered her strength and began to look like a normal, healthy teenager but her clothes were looking shabbier and shabbier until they were hanging off her like rags. Alan Edwards was determined to do something about her appearance.

'Sara, I'm going to make you look the belle of the ball. Just you wait.'

Alan disappeared one morning. Of all the British prisoners of war he was the most daring and his friends worried that he sometimes took too many risks. But there was no stopping Alan, for the greater the risk the greater his sense of triumph.

Just after midday Alan arrived back at the stables, his army greatcoat bulging in one or two unusual places. 'Now, my dear, I can't pretend that you're going to be the height of fashion but here's one or two little numbers I've managed to capture from the enemy.'

He fished inside the greatcoat and produced a sweater and a skirt, presenting them to Sara with a great flourish as if he just performed a conjuring trick. 'Hey presto!' he exclaimed and then added, 'The show's not over yet, folks.'

This time he dug deep within his pockets and produced a pair of stockings and a pair of shoes. He was still not finished and his fellow prisoners wondered whether he would next produce a rabbit and a string with all the flags of the nations upon it.

'And finally . . . these!' Alan produced a large pair of knickers from the waistbelt of his trousers, waving them in the air and then blushing with embarrassment. Sara clasped her hands over her mouth as the rest of the soldiers roared with laughter.

'How did you do it?' asked Sam in disbelief.

'Best not to ask, old boy,' replied Alan in an imitation of an upper-class detective. 'Terribly hush hush. Undercover work. Plain clothes operation.'

Despite her terrible treatment at the hands of the SS guards, Sara's confidence in other non-Jewish people was being gradually restored. But this safe and happy interlude in her life was not to last. Alan Edwards was the first to break the news.

'Just heard from Wilhelm. The Ruskies are breaking through and the Germans are retreating further westwards and they'll be taking us with them.'

The news was devastating to Sara. They could not possibly take her with them, for whilst the guards turned a blind eye to small matters there was no way they would allow a Jewess to accompany them back into Germany.

'What are we to do with Sara?' Stan asked the others. All their faces showed disappointment. No one could come up with an answer to their dilemma except the ever-resourceful Alan Edwards.

'I know one of the Polish lads here. I think he might be able to help.'

Alan left and came back a couple of hours later explaining that his Polish workmate would come after they left and hide her on a nearby farm until the Russians arrived. It was the best plan they could come up with.

The next day they said their goodbyes to Sara and hid her in the false wall next to the chimney. As the trap-door closed on Sara, they all silently prayed for the safety of the girl they'd nursed back to health. Dejected and sad, they fell into rank and marched off from the barn, leaving their precious Sara behind.

After the friendship and kindness Sara had known for a brief time the parting brought an unbearable sense of loneliness and separation. She cried and cried as the short day deepened into night. She listened attentively to every rustle, thinking that Alan's Polish friend was about to arrive. No one came and her despair grew as the grey light of dawn began to steal through the wooden joints of the trapdoor. She had been abandoned!

She could not stay hidden and needed to find food and help. Opening the trapdoor, she climbed down the ladder into the stable. She opened the barn door and took her first steps into the dangerous outside world from which she'd been in hiding.

Sara was saved by a strange stroke of luck. After being arrested and then released by the local police she begged for a job from a local farmer, Heinrich Binder. She was not to know, but this man was the leader of the local Nazis and ordinarily would have turned her in or even killed her. But the Germans were on the run and most were thinking of nothing else but saving their own skins. Binder wanted to flee to Cologne to escape the Russians but knew the Allies would arrest and imprison him so he struck a deal with Sara. He would give her a job and in return she would write on a postcard in Yiddish how he had helped her.

For a while Sara was under the protection of a man who a few months earlier would not have hesitated to kill her. Eventually, Binder fled just before the Russians arrived. It took two more adventurous months, during which time she was arrested by the Russians as a spy, before Sara reached the safety of the town of Bialystok. It was here that she learned that her sister and mother had not survived the death march and, in memory of her sister, added the name of Hannah to her own.

In 1947 she emigrated to New York where she became a nurse and later married.

Reunited

Hannah Sara never forgot the kindness of those British prisoners of war and as the years passed the determination grew in her to meet them again. She wanted to show them that she had survived and that all their efforts had not been in vain. In 1964, with the help of the War Office, she traced Alan Edwards, who was running a car hire fleet in Morecambe. In turn, Alan contacted the remaining nine and eight years later she was reunited with them all in London. Those ten ordinary men had taken huge risks to protect the girl and their courage had triumphed. To Sara they were her brothers in humanity.

This is not quite the end of the story, for the ten were to be honoured by Israel, the state founded by and for

Jewish people. In March 1989 they were invited to Jerusalem but only five were able to make the journey. Four had died and a fifth was too old to make the journey. In Israel, the other five old soldiers, proud in their regimental blazers and ties, planted a carob tree in the Avenue of the Righteous, reserved for those who had risked their lives for Jewish people. Sara, their little sister, stood in their midst, feeling as safe and secure as the day she'd been found and brought to their barracks by Sam Wells.

FIGHTING FACTS

German Scapegoats

After losing World War I many Germans felt frustrated that their country was no longer a strong, powerful nation. When the German economy collapsed in 1929–33, causing widespread poverty and unemployment, some Germans began to look around for someone to blame. Many Jews were successful scientists, writers and bankers, and because of this and because they had different beliefs from many Germans there was a strong anti-Semitic feeling in Germany. Hitler used this to his advantage, turning the Jewish population into scapegoats and blaming them for Germany's ruin.

The Nazis were racists who believed that some races were better than others. According to the Nazis, the

A sign reading: Jews not wanted in this place.
They were put up all over Germany.

'Ayran' race was the 'master race'. The ideal Ayran was a white person with blond hair and blue eyes. They also believed that one's race determined your position in society and how you behaved. As a consequence, Nazis felt that all Jews belonged to an 'inferior race'.

Laws Against the Jews

When the Nazi party came to power in 1933 they began to pass laws against the Jews. These gradually restricted their lives more and more, from not being able to attend the same school as 'Ayrans', to having to wear a yellow star on your clothes, identifying you as a Jew. Everybody's family were examined to see if they had Jewish grandparents because the Nazis were determined to classify everyone.

These laws were the first steps in the horrific final outcome of the Nazis' persecution of the Jews – mass execution in concentration camps.

Protecting Jewish People

When Hitler conquered European countries, they were made to pass anti-Jewish laws. Some governments cooperated, such as in occupied France, but others resisted. The Danish government refused to hand over its Jewish population.

Many individuals risked their lives by hiding Jews. The most famous case is that of the people who hid Anne Frank and her family until they were betrayed. Even some Germans played their part. Oscar Schindler, a factory boss, gave jobs to Jewish workers so as to protect them from being transported to concentration camps.

To Madagascar

In July 1940 the Germans began to discuss a plan to send all the Jewish people to the island of Madagascar off the African coast. This was a French colony but as Germany had conquered France and they had no colonies themselves it was thought they could use this island as a dumping ground. As the war went on this 'solution' to the 'Jewish problem' became impossible, for it meant travelling thousands of miles through Allied lines.

The Final Solution

By 1939 nearly 525,000 people officially defined as 'non-Ayrans' had left Germany. 1941 was a turning point. By then the Nazis had conquered much of Europe and many of the people living in the newly conquered countries were non-Ayrans. For example, over three million Jews lived in Poland. As soon as the Nazis conquered Poland Jews were rounded up and forced to live in enclosed areas or 'ghettos'.

As the Nazi conquest spread into Russia, more and more so-called 'inferior races' fell into German hands. In October 1941 Himmler, the head of the SS, gave orders for a 'final solution' to be put into action. Special camps were set up – death camps, with gas chambers. By the end of the war between **4–6 million people** had been killed in this way, including Jews, gypsies, political prisoners and homosexuals.

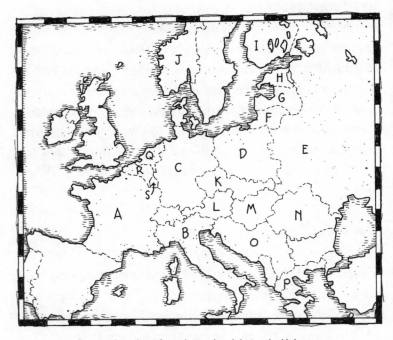

Estimated number of people murdered during the Holocaust.

Key

A France 77,320	E Soviet Union 1,000,000–1,100,000	J Norway 762	O Yugoslavia 56,200–63,300
B Italy 7,680	F Lithuania 140,000–143,000	K Czechoslovakia 150,000	P Greece 60,000–67,000
C Germany 134,500–141,500	G Latvia 70,000–71,500	L Austria 50,000	Q Netherlands 100,000
D Poland 2,900,000–3,000,000	H Estonia 1,500–2,000	M Hungary 550,000–569,000	R Belgium 28,900
	I Finland 7	N Romania 271,000–287,000	S Luxembourg 1,950

Justice

At the end of the war it was decided to put the leading Nazis on trial for crimes against humanity. Hitler, Goebbels (the Minister for Propaganda) and Himmler had already committed suicide. All three had played an important part in bringing about the Final Solution.

After the war, 22 leading Nazis were put on trial in Nuremburg in Germany. They were found guilty and either hanged or given long jail sentences. Over the next twenty years 20,000 people were convicted by either German or Allied courts for crimes committed during the war.

GLOSSARY

anti-Semitic – hostile to the Jewish people
Luftwaffe – the German airforce

ACKNOWLEDGEMENTS

Imperial War Museum: p.11 MH6712, p.13 HU36236 p.15 HU36208, p.17 HU36203, p.18 D26730, p.23 HU52713; Popperfoto: p.102 10002814; Hulton Getty: p.41 M100377, p.48 M100379, p.50 FOXWB6051, p.51 FOXWB6050, p.55 TOP56393, KEY483181, P81068, p.90 FOXWB8321, p.93 FOXW88295, p.99 KEY437918, p.106 M5071; p.127 M134876.

Every effort has been made to trace copyright holders. We would be grateful to hear from any copyright holders not acknowledged here.

A WORLD IN FLAMES
WAR IN THE AIR

Peter Hepplewhite

Six fantastic stories about war in the air during World War II.

In 1940 Stuka dive-bombers pound a Sussex radar station. Will they knock out Britain's warning systems and pave the way for a German invasion?

As the Battle of Britain reaches its height a desperate Hurricane pilot runs out of ammunition. How can he stop a German bomber heading straight for Buckingham Palace?

Deadly Focke-Wulf fighters pounce on a Lancaster bomber over Berlin. Does the stricken plane stand a chance of ever making it home?

Trapped by searing anti-aircraft fire, an American B-17 bomber bursts in flames. Will the courage of one crewman be enough to fight the fire?

Blowing down the walls of Amiens prison to rescue 700 Resistance fighters. Is this a mission impossible for the Mosquito squadrons?

During the summer of 1944 a new weapon blasts London. Can Britain's best fighter pilots stop the sinister V1 flying bombs?

Packed with fighting facts and black and white photographs.

A WORLD IN FLAMES
WAR ON LAND

Neil Tonge

Six fantastic stories about war on land during World War II.

In May 1940, the German army launches its attack on France and sends the British Army reeling back to the coast. How will they get home?

On 23 October 1942, in North Africa, General Montgomery launches his long-anticipated attack on Rommel's army. Has the tide of war finally changed in favour of the Allies?

In September 1943 Pearl Witherington, a British secret agent, parachutes into France to work with the French Resistance. Will she be able to avoid capture by the Gestapo?

As dawn breaks on 6 June 1944 250,000 soldiers storm ashore a 60-mile stretch of beach in Normandy. Will they make it through the longest day of the war?

Operation Market Garden is a daring plan to capture the bridges across the Rhine. What will happen to the troops when it all goes wrong?

By May 1942 all of Burma is in Japanese hands and they are poised to strike into India. Can the British army hold them back and recapture Burma?

Packed with fighting facts and black and white photographs.

A WORLD IN FLAMES
WAR AT SEA

Peter Hepplewhite

Six fantastic stories about war at sea during World War II.

On 5 November 1940, Convoy HX 84 is attacked by the German battleship *Admiral Scheer*. Can the liner *Jervis Bay* buy enough time to save the convoy?

A week later in the Mediterranean, the Fleet Air Arm attack Italian battleships in Taranto harbour. Will 21 dated Swordfish dive-bombers be up to the job?

The fearsome battleship, the *Bismarck*, slips out of the Baltic in May 1941. Can the Royal Navy catch her before she escapes to ravage British convoys?

Convoy OB 318 is attacked by the German submarine *U-110*. The escorts fight back. Can they go a step further and capture her precious code books?

In August 1942 Canadian troops lead an assault on the town of Dieppe. It goes horribly wrong. Can the Navy get its men home?

In the autumn of 1943, as cold winds begin to bite in the Arctic circle, the X-craft strike. But will they be able to cripple the battleship *Tirpitz*?

Packed with fighting facts and black and white photographs.

Collect all A WORLD IN FLAMES books

The prices shown below are correct at the time of going to press.
However, Macmillan Publishers reserve the right to show new retail
prices on covers which may differ from those previously advertised.

A World in Flames	Peter Hepplewhite and Neil Tonge	
At Sea	0 330 48295 5	£4.99
In the Air	0 330 48296 3	£4.99
On Land	0 330 48294 7	£4.99
Civilians	0 330 48297 1	£4.99

All Macmillan titles can be ordered at your local bookshop
or are available by post from:

**Book Service by Post
PO Box 29, Douglas, Isle of Man IM99 1BQ**

Credit cards accepted. For details:
Telephone: 01624 675137
Fax: 01624 670923
E-mail: bookshop@enterprise.net

Free postage and packing in the UK.
Overseas customers: add £1 per book (paperback)
and £3 per book (hardback).